The LAW SCHOOL BIBLE

The
LAW SCHOOL BIBLE

How Anyone Can Become A Lawyer...
Without Ever Setting Foot In A Law School!
... unless you really want to

By

Peter J. Loughlin, Esq., J.D., LL.M.

Marilux Press

Naples, Florida

Printed and bound in the United States of America

ISBN 0-9710281-0-9

Published by:
Marilux Press
2338 Immokalee Road, No. 162
Naples, Florida 34110-1445
Email: sales@MariluxPress.com

TESTIMONIALS

"I thought going to law school was just a dream, but in one month I was able to turn my unfocused desire to change careers into matriculation at a high-quality distance-learning law school. All without having to quit my job and moving my family to another city. I didn't even need to complete my Bachelors Degree or take the LSAT. Peter J. Loughlin saved me years, and easily over $100,000 in student loans. You can't afford not to get this book."

- Kelley Richmond Harvey, Law Student, Nashville, TN

"I am ecstatic, thrilled, happy, excited, and it's all due to that 'Great Book,' The Law School Bible, which I purchased from you a couple months back. I would have never imagined I would someday be saying that I have been accepted to a law school to earn a law degree. Never in my wildest dreams would I believe this was possible until I bought your book."

- Ron Coculo, Law Student, Fayette, ME

"Congratulations to Professor Peter Loughlin, J.D., LL.M., on the culmination of several years of research and practical involvement in the study of law. Your aim from the outset was to find avenues whereby the study of law was within the reach of the ordinary person. The Law School Bible has more than surpassed that lofty goal, and I am confident that many eager law school prospects will find the sources, so eloquently laid out in this masterful book—their route to achieving their goal of obtaining a law degree."

- Rivington A. Powery, B.A., LL.B., Professor of Law, www.crown-lawcentre.com

"Peter J. Loughlin has done a great service for those individuals who always dreamed about being a lawyer, but for some reason or other, were precluded from getting into law school. Mr. Loughlin's book The Law School Bible is worth its weight in gold for providing a roadmap that explains not only how you can earn a quality law degree without mortgaging your future with student loans, but also shows how you can save thousands of dollars and time to enter the legal profession in the United States, The United Kingdom and in other common law jurisdictions. An invaluable resource for the future lawyer."

- George D. Pappas, Esq., B.Sc.(Econ), LL.B. (Hon), LL.M
Editor & Attorney at Law — The Malet Street Gazette

"Finally there is a book that unravels the mystery of the Bar admissions process."

- Richard Finley, America's Bar Review

"The definitive bible on unconventional law school. This is the best information I have found to date. Peter's writing style is extraordinary. I read the book the 1st time in under 3 hours. It is worth 50 to 100 times the price in the time and money it will save you. It should be on the shelf of every public and educational institution in the country. A must read if you think you want to be a lawyer."

- Bill Julian, Columbia, SC

"I recently received the 'Bible' and I am blown away at the simplicity it takes to become a lawyer without going through the traditional approach of weight gain and loss at the expense of the so- called shapers of the legal minds. I am very impressed with the contents, the simplicity. I would like to thank you for opening my eyes to a whole new experience. It would be a privilege to subscribe to your newsletter. Thank you!"

- Nicholas Lake, Staten Island, NY

"If it hadn't been for The Law School Bible I would still be trying to figure out how to become a lawyer—sure I'm not one yet, but at least I saved three years of additional studies that really weren't necessary. Thanks to The Law School Bible (and Dr. Loughlin) I've been able to search for an adequate ABA school (for my LL.M), and now... I graduate next September, ready to take the Bar...Thank you very much!!"

- Anthony Lewis, Walhalla, SC

"The Law School Bible is an invaluable resource for anyone considering a law degree. I devoured it cover to cover and found that it delivered everything Peter Loughlin promised and so much more. Peter also gave generously of his time, providing me with a personal consultation by phone. He says he enjoys helping people and his genuineness shows."

- Tim Masters, Rochester, NY

"I read this book and I now believe that I too can be a lawyer. Mr. Loughlin's personal story let's you know that if you are willing to do the work you can achieve just about anything. The book also comes with a great deal of practical advice as well as invaluable lists of where to go to get the information you need. It is totally comprehensive and complete in telling you exactly what to do to become an attorney without traditional law school. Amazing book!"

- Tony Books Avilez, New York, NY

"Peter Loughlin has been my personal law-school guru for the past three years. His insight and expertise have been priceless resources in my journey to the Bar. This book is a must read for anyone even remotely contemplating a legal career."

- Warren J. Werbe, CPA, J.D., LL.M.

"When it comes to alternative legal education, Peter Loughlin wrote the book, and I recommend you buy it now!"

- Steve D. Kent, B.S.L., J.D.

This book is dedicated to my wife, Ewa, my sons PJ,
Brian and Christopher and, Mom and Dad for all the
times I was locked away in my office studying law,
researching this book and seemingly forgot you—
I did not. Thank you for your tireless support
and belief in me.

If you attack the establishment long enough and hard
enough, they will make you a member of it.

Art Buchwald

CONTENTS

THE
LAW SCHOOL
BIBLE

But small is the gate and narrow the road that leads to life, and only a few find it
—Matthew 7:14

Two roads diverged in a wood, and I—I took the one less traveled by, and that has made all the difference.
—Robert Frost

INTRODUCTION

Many books have been written on the topic of nontraditional or alternative education but few have focused on the opportunity to utilize these methods to obtain a professional law degree. Rare is the person who has not heard of such things as correspondence courses, home study or distance learning, however, many persons are not quite sure how to maximize the advantages provided by alternative education. It is ironic that the explosive growth experienced by the industry has itself caused much of the apprehension and confusion that prevents potential lawyers from reaching their academic and career goals. It is the sheer number of choices of schools and academic programs that has caused many to be caught up in this mysterious system, often not knowing which way to turn for help.

This book takes the mystery out of alternative legal education and removes many of the risks that result from poor planning and misinformation. For example, a number of alternative and distance-learning law programs boast of being "accredited." At one point in time this claim may have had some real meaning, however, today there are literally thousands of so-called accrediting agencies worldwide. Many of these agencies are valid in their own limited fields of influence, but quite a large number of them are self-serving and, for most purposes, worthless. I have heard many horror stories from people who have spent four years or more working toward a law degree only to learn that the degree will not be acceptable to employers or professional bar associations. Sadly, the education they received may have, in fact, been outstanding, but it is nonetheless useless for the purposes intended—to practice law.

All of the law-degree programs listed in this book have one thing in common, they are alternative programs. That is, they are not traditional in that you will generally NOT be required to take standardized entrance examinations such as the LSAT to gain admission to them.

Most programs will, however, require that you have met some minimum educational requirements or specific coursework prior to being accepted into the program, all of which can also be acquired nontraditionally. The beauty of taking the alternative route to your professional law degree is that you will not be shut out by quotas or other artificial barriers that have excluded so many potential lawyers—perhaps even you— from achieving the dream of becoming a lawyer.

Interestingly enough, the programs and strategies outlined in this book are only considered nontraditional from a U.S. perspective. As you will learn, distance learning law-degree programs are actually quite common and highly respected in other common law countries throughout the world. You will also learn that the strategies presented here are made possible because the United States follows the common law of England, as does Canada, Australia, Ireland, and most Caribbean and many Asian and African nations— and, of course, the United Kingdom. U.S. case law is still derived from and, to some extent, tied directly to England, and, American courts rely heavily on past and present English case law. English courts also cite American cases with great regularity. It is this strong nexus, this common and "globally" accepted common-law legal system that makes the strategies of this book possible.

Law students, whether they are studying in the United States, England, Canada, Australia, the Caribbean and most of the current and former commonwealth nations, will, with few exceptions, study the exact same legal principles. Yes, that's right, aside from some distinctions in procedure and constitutional differences, law students in these countries will study nearly identical course material. Furthermore, if you choose, you need never leave your own hometown to study at a foreign law school because foreign law schools have had well respected and accredited distance-learning programs for nearly two centuries. However, don't be misled by the seemingly open-door policy of the alternative law-degree programs, all are extremely demanding to say the very least. These alternatives provide you with an opportunity to prove that you can make it—but making it is entirely up to you.

You should be aware from the very beginning that you will have to make changes in your life and dedicate a good deal of time for your studies. Family support will be vital to your success. You will be required to work very hard and, when you think you've been pushed to your limits, you will have to give some more. Cast aside any illusions that this is a shortcut to becoming a lawyer; it is nothing of the kind. To become a lawyer you must undertake a demanding, thorough, and complete course of study. There are no shortcuts.

If you think about it for a moment, I'm sure you'll agree that your professional education *should* be demanding, thorough and complete. Would you want to be represented by a lawyer with substandard training, treated by an incompetent doctor or have your tax planning done by a bungling CPA? Of course not, that is why I have only selected law programs that are accredited, registered or approved by recognized professional or academic bodies. In short, if you came here looking for a bogus diploma to hang on your wall or to impress your friends with, you came to the wrong place. Here, you will be asked to roll up your sleeves, dust off the old gray matter and get ready to take a journey. Your journey will be demanding but if you persevere your success will be most rewarding. You *can* achieve your dream of being a lawyer.

If you think you have what it takes to become a lawyer and you are not afraid to work hard to prove it, you can fulfill your dreams of becoming a lawyer through alternative legal education.

How To Use This Book

This book was written to serve as a directory and comprehensive guide to alternative legal education. Although various methods of nontraditional legal education have been around for close to 200 years, in recent decades they have been cast into the nether regions where only those fortunate enough to stumble upon them by chance or find them by diligent investigation have been able to benefit from them. The vast majority of the population, particularly in the United States, has never been exposed to alternative pathways to becoming a lawyer.

If this is your first exposure to alternative legal education, I strongly recommend that you read this book in its entirety. Take your time and get a flavor for the breadth of this topic and the many strategies available to you. Once you have done this, then go back and focus on those chapters that offer the strategies and options that appeal to you and best fit your particular circumstances. Make full use of the school directories. The directories were placed in this book to provide a complete repository of nearly every (if not every) non-American Bar Association school in the United States and law schools of every major common law country in the world. No other book or directory (online or offline) has ever assembled all of these resources in one place single place.

If you're already familiar with alternative legal education, this book will serve as a valued resource. You can use *The Law School Bible* as your personal reference book. It will provide you with valuable contacts for law schools, bar associations, tutorial programs and, as a guide for the "rules of the game."

Naturally the resources and contact information provided here may change from time to time, however, by registering as a reader of this book you will be able to stay on top of any changes in contact information, and, more importantly, receive critical updates about bar admission policies. To register you will need to send an e-mail to:

register@LawSchoolBible.com.

Our wrangling lawyers . . . are so litigious and busy here on earth, that I think they will plead their clients' causes hereafter—some of them in hell.
—Robert Burton

Chapter I

Can You Really Become a Lawyer Without Going to an ABA Approved or Accredited Law School?

In 2003 ABA law schools experienced a 17% rise in applications. And, more than 133,000 prospective law students have taken the grueling Law School Admissions Test, better known as the LSAT. Of those 133,000, a little over 80,000 will make applications to attend an ABA law school. Of the 80,000 applicants to ABA law schools only about 25% will ever be admitted and less than 50% of those students will ever graduate and be admitted to practice law. Although the weeding-out process is intense, the number of applicants continues to increase from year to year and there is no indication that this widespread interest in becoming a lawyer will ever decline.

So why does "everyone" want to be a lawyer? Lawyers are a respected and much needed group of professionals. You may have heard that there is a glut of lawyers and that the laws schools have churned out too many law graduates, all competing with you in an ever-narrowing job market—don't believe it! While it may be true that the United States has an overwhelming number of lawyers in comparison to other countries, it is equally true that we live in an extraordinarily litigious society. It is estimated that one in three Americans will be involved in a lawsuit during his or her lifetime and there is no indication that this trend will decrease any time soon. Remember also that this one in three potential client ratio represents only a small area of practice for lawyers. Additional areas of legal practice include the following:

Criminal Law   Federal Practice
Contracts   Wills and Trust Law

Personal Injury	Elder Law
Constitutional Law	Tax Law
Administrative Law	International Law
Real Estate Law	Immigration Law
Environmental Law	Bankruptcy Law
Family Law	Intellectual Property

This list is not by any means exhaustive and while some lawyers opt to specialize in a particular area of law others take a more generalist approach to the practice of law.

Perhaps an even more convincing reason for becoming a lawyer is that a lawyer is not limited to the practice of law. Quite frankly having a law degree opens the door to career opportunities in a wide variety of fields. Lawyers are in demand in management, banking, finance, sales, import-export, communications and, of course, teaching. There is no limit to the cross-career prospects for lawyers.

> *"Perhaps an even more convincing reason for becoming a lawyer is that a lawyer is not limited to the practice of law. Quite frankly having a law degree opens the door to career opportunities in a wide variety of fields."*

As Abraham Lincoln stated, achieving your dream of becoming a lawyer is often more a product of your state of mind and your level of tenacity than it is any other factor. If you can obtain your legal education in the traditional manner, that is, taking the LSATs and getting admitted to an ABA law school, I encourage you to do so. You will obtain an outstanding education to be sure. But that does not mean that an equally outstanding legal education cannot be obtained by other means. Some nontraditional law schools and their graduates boast a higher pass rate on the Bar Exam than graduates of traditional law schools. Many non-ABA U.S. and foreign law schools are world renowned for their law programs. The University of London, for example, has a highly respected external law-degree program that requires external students to be tested on the exact same standard as internal students. The examinations are offered in every major city in the world. Because the testing standard is the same for internal and external students, all graduates of such programs can rightly be proud of their outstanding legal education.

Disadvantages of Traditional Law Schools

There are a number of reasons why so many prospective law students are turning their backs to traditional American legal education. For some, the problems of going to an ABA law school are just not worth it, especially considering that an excellent legal education can be achieved by other means. The fact is that going to an ABA law school is not for everyone. Going the traditional route is just not practical or desirable for a variety of reasons, for instance:

- ABA Law Schools are very expensive (the average cost is about $30,000.00 per year) Note: Tuition for full-time students rose 8.6% in 2004.
- Inflexible class schedules
- The general requirement of a bachelor's degree
- The general requirement of an undergraduate GPA of 3.5 or higher
- The general requirement of high LSAT scores
- Location (Most law schools are only located in major cities)

> *"...achieving your dream of becoming a lawyer is often more a product of your state of mind and your level of tenacity than it is any other factor."*

Advantages of Alternative Legal Education

The above reasons form a formidable and impenetrable barrier for some prospective lawyers—and a dream killer for many others. But you don't have to give up your dream. Many of the problems associated with going to a traditional law school are easily overcome by the many benefits of nontraditional legal education. Those benefits are numerous and can often mean the difference between attaining your goal or always wondering what might have been. Let's take a look at some of the many benefits of nontraditional legal education:

- Low Cost (Often less than $5,000 per year)
- Flexible Class schedules (online, correspondence, nights and weekends)
- Bachelor's degree normally not required
- GPA is often irrelevant
- Normally no LSATs are required
- Location (there are many online and correspondence programs available)
- An excellent legal education

As you can see, the so-called alternative route can often offer many more benefits than the traditional route. Many individuals often choose the nontraditional path, not because they cannot go to an ABA law school, but rather because, on balance, it is much more attractive.

CASE STUDY

Please indulge me for a moment, while I use myself as an example of what can be accomplished through alternative legal education. You see, I've actually utilized nearly every strategy discussed in this book, and I think I make a good case study.

I always wanted to be a lawyer, but my dream had to be put on hold because I married at the tender age of 19 and, over the next 20 years, found myself raising my three wonderful boys. I don't regret for a moment that I had family obligations, that was a choice I made—a wonderful choice. During those years I held several positions with the New York City municipal government, including that of police lieutenant. It was during my tenure in law enforcement that my dream of becoming a lawyer was revived, but I had a major barrier standing in my way, I did not have any college credits.

I knew I would have to get a college degree first before even thinking about law school, but I did not want to wait four years for a Bachelor's degree. (I later learned that there were methods available that didn't require an undergraduate degree). I was fortunate to learn about a system called "testing out." Testing out is basically studying college courses at home and then taking examinations for accredited college credit. It isn't as easy as it sounds, but it does work very well if you cannot commit to a regular class schedule. And the education you'll receive can be remarkably good. Working with the police, my work shift was subject to frequent changes, so there was just no way I could attend regular classes at the local college. After about two years of "testing out" I earned enough credits for a B.A. degree and applied my credits for graduation at Regents College, a fully accredited university in New York State (now called Excelsior College). It is also a great way to save thousands of dollars over the cost of a traditional college degree. To learn more about testing out, visit **www.MaxStudy.com**.

Even though I worked extremely hard at my studies and scored well in my examinations, for some strange reason I had a sense that my education was somehow tainted or lacking. I wanted to know that I was at least equal to those who earned their degree through traditional education, so what I did was to enroll in a traditional Master's degree program just to see if I was really good enough. Well, with a 3.9 GPA, I guess I felt that my nontraditional education *was* good enough and I was now validated—OK, I supposed, I might now humbly try to get into law school—any law school.

When I first began to research law schools, I was shocked by the cost and the incredibly complex admissions' process with the Law School Admissions Test, GPAs, and most frightening of all, those huge student loans that I would need to pay off. I mean, it would be like taking on another mortgage, wouldn't it? I began to think about my undergraduate education and thought, "wouldn't it be great if I could obtain a law degree by distance learning." It would, and I soon learned about California's distance-learning law schools and I enrolled in one, Saratoga University School of Law. Now mind you, Saratoga is not approved by the American Bar Association (ABA) or accredited in the traditional sense, but it is registered with the State Bar of California and it is authorized to confer the Juris Doctor degree. More importantly, its graduates may sit for the general bar examination.

While I was studying for my Juris Doctor degree, I learned about the University of London External Programme, a fully accredited law school offering law degrees by distance learning. I thought it might be nice, though not necessary, to work toward an accredited law degree, so I cross-registered there to supplement my studies at Saratoga. The combined cost of enrollment in both universities was less than $4,000.00 per year.

After I graduated from Saratoga in May of 2000 I enrolled in an LL.M program in International Taxation at St Thomas University School of Law, an ABA approved law school. I did this for two reasons, 1) my own self-validation concerns about my unaccredited law degree and, 2) I confess to being one of those geeks who loves crunching numbers, but that's another story.

What did all of this do for me? Quite simply it fulfilled my lifelong dream of being a lawyer. I passed the Bar examination and have published legal articles on international taxation and Immigration Law that were well received in the professional community. I established my own rewarding law practice and was hired as an adjunct professor of Law. But all of this pales in comparison to the enjoyment and fulfillment I receive working as a legal-education consultant helping others like you to fulfill their dreams of becoming a lawyer. Not too bad considering this was all just a dream a few years ago.

That's enough about me. I must tell you that while I love and believe in alternative legal education, I admit that I am biased, and quite frankly you might even question my using myself as an example of what can be achieved through the strategies discussed in this book. After all, maybe I was just lucky, right? Well, I do consider myself lucky, but just so you will know that I am not alone, I have peppered this book with case studies of other "lucky" people so that you will know that you too can be lucky—if you're willing to work hard.

Can you really become a lawyer
without going to an ABA law school?
—Absolutely!

If you are resolutely determined to make a lawyer of yourself, the thing is more than half done already. It is but a small matter whether you read with anybody or not. I did not read with anyone. Get the books and read and study them until you understand them and their principle features; and that is the main thing. It is of no consequence to be in a large town while you are reading. I read in Salem, which never had three hundred people living in it. The books and your capacity for understanding them are just the same in all places. Always bear in mind that your resolution to succeed is more important than any other one thing.
—Abraham Lincoln

Chapter II

Traditional vs. Alternative Routes to Becoming a Lawyer

Many guidebooks and manuals have been written to assist candidates to enter the practice of law. These books tend to focus on the traditional pathways to a career in law. Although this book takes a focused look at alternative methods of becoming a member of the legal profession, we will briefly discuss the conventional methods in order to draw a comparison between the two approaches.

Traditional Routes to Becoming a Lawyer in the United States

Bachelor's Degree

With rare practical exception, traditional law-school candidates in the United States must have earned a bachelor's degree (in any field) from an accredited college or university. Some law schools may make exceptions, subject to certain regulations, and consider a candidate with less than a bachelor's degree or its equivalent. However, this is not a realistic strategy and not one that I would recommend. By and large, you must have a bachelor's degree from an accredited college or university before your application will be considered by an ABA law school.

Grade Point Average

Not only must the traditional law-school hopefuls earn a bachelor's degree or its equivalent, but they also must generally have done so with an acceptable Grade Point Average, more commonly known as GPA. The individual ABA-approved law schools establish the acceptable GPA minimum, which may be as low as 3.0 but is more likely to be 3.5 or higher. While it is true that there is a small degree of flexibility permitted by admissions' committees when considering a candidate's overall qualifications, do not expect too many exceptions. With so many applicants and so few seats, admissions' committees do not need to make many exceptions, nor are they inclined to do so.

The problem with concentrating on a candidate's GPA is that, quite frankly, many college students, due to immaturity, or career or family commitments, have failed to truly apply themselves properly while in college. This means that while the GPA is indicative of how the candidate has performed in the past, it may not necessarily provide an accurate idea of his present or future ability. Still, once your GPA has been set, it will be difficult to convince admissions' committees from ABA law schools that you have matured and changed. Why should they believe you? Why should they give you a chance? I'm sorry to tell you that they probably will not.

Law School Admission Test

The cornerstone of the traditional law-school admissions process starts with the candidate's earning an acceptable score on the Law School Admission Test (LSAT). The acceptable minimum LSAT scores varies which each individual law school and most law schools will, to some degree, allow for some consideration of a candidate's overall ability and suitability. However, make no mistake about it, a substandard score on the LSAT will substantially reduce your chances of getting into a traditional ABA law school.

Let's face it, space is limited and it is expensive to run a high-quality law school, staffed by a qualified faculty with an extensive library and support staff. Law schools are obligated to try and weed out anyone who might not make it. Why? First of all, though unfair to the candidate, if the student failure rate is too high it reflects poorly on the school's performance and ranking and ultimately the "bottom line" when it comes to attracting new qualified applicants. The bottom line is important to ABA law schools for many reasons, and they're not all economic. For one thing, whatever few stones can be cast at the rigidity of the ABA law-school system, you have to admit that you generally cannot fault them on academic grounds. ABA law schools offer very high quality legal education, period. But to maintain such high standards they must weed out the weak candidates. The system tolerates few exceptions.

This weeding out of borderline or unqualified candidates is an absolute necessity for these schools. There is, for the most part, nothing personal about the weeding-out process, but the problem is that some high-quality people just don't make the cut. Rest assured, the study of law is not for everyone, but if you are one of the qualified few who did not make the cut (or just could not afford to go the traditional road), take heart, there are some alternative approaches to becoming a lawyer.

> *"With so many applicants and so few seats, admissions' committees do not need to make many exceptions, nor are they inclined to do so."*

Alternative Routes to Becoming a Lawyer in the United States

The American Bar Association and Law School Accreditation

Before we move ahead, a few more things about the American Bar Association (ABA) require a bit of explaining. The ABA is a private professional association that engages in a wide range of functions on behalf of its members. One of these functions is to establish minimum standards by which American law schools are to be guided. If a particular U.S. law school elects to be governed by the ABA standards, that school may voluntarily seek "approval" of the ABA. ABA approval is a much coveted and respected status indeed. Prospective lawyers wishing to attend an ABA law school <u>must</u> comply with the strict traditional requirements of becoming a lawyer.

The majority of law schools in the United States are ABA approved, however, some schools cannot meet the stringent standards of the ABA. A small number of non-ABA law schools in the U.S. are excellent, but choose not to seek ABA approval. The general rule in the U.S. is that only graduates of ABA-approved law schools may sit for bar examinations and ultimately become lawyers. However, as with most general rules there are exceptions. There are in fact a number of U.S. states that permit law graduates from foreign or U.S. non-ABA law schools to sit for their bar examinations.

> *"The general rule in the U.S. is that only graduates of ABA-approved law schools may sit for bar examinations and ultimately become lawyers. However, as with most general rules there are exceptions."*

The ABA serves merely in an advisory capacity and the individual states are free to establish their own requirements. That being said, you should also know that this "advisory" role has proven to be quite powerful and far reaching—every U.S. state permits graduates of ABA law schools to sit for their bar examination. But some states will also permit graduates of non-ABA approved law schools to sit for the exam as well. Normally these schools have sought and obtained "state approval" or have met other requirements of the state bar, for example, being "registered" with the State Bar Association.

Foreign Law School Accreditation

The accreditation process outside of the United States is generally administered by governmental bodies. In this respect ABA approval is not relevant to the accreditation status of foreign law schools.

Law in America evolved directly from the common law of England and from our common heritage. For this reason, quite a number of U.S. states will permit foreign law graduates to sit for their bar exam if their education was based upon English common law and is substantially equivalent to American ABA-law school education. Note that the standard is "substantially equivalent" and not the exact equivalent. By and large the legal education obtained from accredited foreign law schools in countries following the common law of England, will be the substantial equivalent of an ABA-law school education.

Alternative Strategies

These features of the American legal education system have created a number of alternative strategies for becoming a lawyer in the United States. Essentially these strategies will involve your doing one of the following:

- Attending and earning a degree from a foreign accredited law school, or
- Enrolling in and earning a degree from a foreign accredited distance-learning law school, or
- Attending and earning a degree from a U.S. non-ABA approved law school, or
- Enrolling in and earning a degree from a U.S. distance-learning law school

> *"...if you are one of the qualified few who did not make the cut (or just could not afford to go the traditional road), take heart, there are some alternative approaches to becoming a lawyer."*

What are the Prerequisites to Attending a Foreign or Nontraditional Law School?

The admission requirements for the alternative law-degree programs will vary from program to program but most will require one of the following academic prerequisites:

- 60 credits from an accredited college or university, or equivalent
- 60 credits from college level examination (e.g., CLEP), or
- bachelor's degree from an accredited college or university, or
- completion of "A"&"O" level examinations (for foreign students)
- meeting the requirements for mature student status

As discussed above, most American law schools will require that candidates for admission have completed an accredited bachelor's degree or its equivalent. Although some ABA law schools indicate that they will accept students with two or three years of college study, very few, if any, students will be accepted without first earning a bachelor's degree. The same is true of most Canadian law schools in that they may state that a bachelor's degree is not required for admission, but rarely is a student admitted without one.

Furthermore, many of the English, Irish, and Australian law schools listed in this book do not require a prior college degree. They, instead, will require that the student either successfully complete their "A" and "O" level examinations. (These are examinations that are taken in the UK and some other Commonwealth nations and are not required for U.S. and other "foreign" students.) Alternatively, these schools will admit students if that student is a "mature" candidate, that is, that he or she be over 21 years of age and be able to demonstrate their academic promise through work or life experience.

Although there are no hard and fast rules as to how liberal foreign law schools will be in accepting a "mature" student, gaining admission will generally be much easier for students with some work experience (not necessarily in law) and/or some education above the high-school level. Furthermore, it is generally, but not always, easier to gain entry into a distance-learning law school. Therefore, if you're set on physically attending a foreign law school, and you're having problems qualifying for admission, you may want to consider doing your first year by distance learning and later reapplying for actual attendance study.

Finally, there are the American non-ABA approved law schools. The norm is to require the student to have 60 college credits or their equivalent. This is particularly true where the student intends to become a practicing lawyer. For example, in California, where most non-accredited law schools are located, law students intending to seek admission to the Bar must have at least 60 college credits or its equivalent by testing out, that is, earning credit by examination, for example by taking CLEP examinations. This is true whether you physically attend an unaccredited law school or enroll in an American distance-learning law school. In short, if you intend to practice law you <u>must</u> have 60 college credits or equivalent. For more information about CLEP and other credit by examination programs please visit: **www.MaxStudy.com**.

A Brief Word About Testing Out

By a procedure known as testing out, many students earn their entire 60 credits or more. In fact, you can actually earn an accredited Associate, Bachelor, or Master's degree without ever setting foot in a college or university—you can even earn a PhD—and, of course, a law degree.

Incidentally, I "tested out" and personally took over a dozen CLEP and similar examinations about 20 years ago. I was fortunate to learn and develop some great study skills, but I must confess that I did waste valuable time studying areas that CLEP didn't even test. I would have paid almost anything to have some good test prep material like those available from **Instant Cert University at www.MaxStudy.com**. I like their program because it uses a question-based learning process, something I've promoted for years—because it works. I also like and endorse this program because you get to try it for 30 days risk free

Testing out is a wonderful way to earn college credits quickly—and cheaply. Essentially a typical testing out student will purchase books and/or other study materials designed to prepare students for examinations in a host of subjects. The examinations are given on a monthly basis in nearly every major city in the United States and throughout the world. The study materials have been developed over the past 30 years or so and are prepared to save the student a lot of wasted time by focusing on exactly what is necessary to prepare for the exams. Nearly all colleges and universities accept the results of these examinations for college credit at their institutions. Additionally you can save thousands of dollars over the cost of a traditional college education by using the testing out system.

For information on books and programs about testing out and CLEP, see Appendix D.

Why must your pre-law or college degree be accredited?

In a word, accreditation equals "acceptance." Ironically, while not all the alternative law-degree programs are themselves accredited in the traditional sense, you must demonstrate that you are academically qualified to enter the programs. This is because graduating from one of the alternative law-degree programs will ultimately qualify you and permit you to sit for the licensing examination and join the Bar Association.

In the United States there are literally hundreds of independent and often competitive accrediting bodies that purport to have the authority to grant accreditation to colleges. This is not always the case and you must therefore be careful that your college degree is truly "accredited' by a "recognized body." Fortunately, a central nonprofit organization has come to the forefront to establish a standard of excellence. This organization, the Council for Higher Education Accreditation (CHEA), was created in 1996 by national referendum and serves as the principal organization to maintain public accountability and assurance of high academic quality and integrity.

It is therefore essential that your pre-law school education or degree be accredited by one of the eight regional accreditation organizations that are represented to CHEA as meeting its eligibility standard. There are, of course, some exceptions and overlapping with certain professional bodies which also have a role in approving or accrediting schools and programs. Where such exceptions are relevant, they will be discussed in further detail.

The following are the eight regional accrediting organizations which are represented by CHEA as meeting its eligibility standard:

Middle States Association of Colleges and Schools (MSA)
Commission on Higher Education
3624 Market Street
Philadelphia, PA 19104
Tel: 215-662-5606, Fax: 215-662-5501
E-mail: jmorse@msache.org
Web: http://www.msache.org

New England Association of Schools and Colleges
Commission on Institutions of Higher Education
209 Burlington Road
Bedford, MA 07130-1433
Tel: 781-271-0022, Fax: 781-271-0950
E-mail: ccook@neasc.org
Web: http://www.neasc.org

New England Association of Schools and Colleges
Commission on Technical and Career Institutions
209 Burlington Road
Bedford, MA 01730-1433
Tel: 781-271-0022, Fax: 781-271-0950
E-mail: rmandeville@neasc.org
Web: http://www.neasc.org

North Central Association of Colleges and Schools
Commission on Institutions of Higher Education
30 North LaSalle, Suite 2400
Chicago, IL 60602-2504
Tel: 312-263-0456, Fax: 312-263-7462
E-mail: crow@ncacihe.org
Web: http://www.ncacihe.org

Northwest Association of Schools and Colleges
Commission on Colleges
11130 NE 33rd Place, Suite 120
Bellevue, WA 98004
Tel: 425-827-2005, Fax: 425-827-3395
E-mail: selman@cocnasc.org
Web: http://www.cocnasc.org

Southern Association of Colleges and Schools
Commission on Colleges
1866 Southern Lane
Decatur, GA 30033-4097
Tel: 404-679-4500, Fax: 404-679-4558
E-mail: jrogers@sacscoc.org
Web: http://www.sacscoc.org

Western Association of Schools and Colleges
Accrediting Commission for Community and Junior Colleges
3402 Mendocino Avenue
Santa Rosa, CA 95403-2244
Tel: 707-569-9177, Fax: 707-569-9179
E-mail: ACCJC@aol.com
Web: http://www.wascweb.org

Western Association of Schools and Colleges
Accrediting Commission for Senior Colleges and Universities
985 Atlantic Avenue, Suite 100
Alameda, CA 94501
Tel: 510-748-9001, Fax: 510-748-9797
E-mail: rwolff@wascsenior.org
Web: http://www.wascweb.org

Legal Accrediting Bodies in the United States

American Bar Association (ABA)
750 N. Lake Shore Drive
Chicago, IL 60611
Tel: 312-988-500
E-mail: Not available
Web: www.abanet.org

Association of American Law Schools (AALS)
1201 Connecticut Ave, N.W., Suite 800
Washington, D.C. 20036-2605
Tel: 202-296-8851, Fax: 202-296-8869
E-mail: Not available
Web: www.aals.org

Accrediting Bodies Outside the United States

In almost all other countries accrediting bodies are a part of or controlled by governmental agencies. For example, in the United Kingdom, university accreditation is by an Act of Parliament. Some strategies described in this book are based on using foreign accredited distance learning and attendance programs. Where this is the case you will normally need to have your "foreign" academic credentials evaluated by academic and professional bodies in the United States. Should you choose one of these strategies, in whole or in part, your credentials may be evaluated by one of the following evaluation services for a cost of approximately $150.00 to $600.00.

Note that the organizations that perform these services are not regulated in the United States. It is strongly suggested that you determine ahead of time whether or not the schools you are interested in will accept the evaluation of these services. Many U.S. schools have the service available for their students—again, check first. Most evaluation services can complete the evaluation report in three to four weeks, however, several firms offer 24-hour service.

Below is a list of companies offering academic evaluation services for foreign college credits and degrees:

Center for Applied Research and Education
P.O. Box 20348
Long Beach, CA 90801
Tel: 562-430-1105, Fax: 562-430-8215
E-Mail: Not Available
Web: Not Available

Educational Credential Evaluators
P.O. Box 92970
Milwaukee, WI 53202
Tel: 414-289-3400, Fax: 414-289-3411
E-mail: eval@ece.org
Web: http://www.ece.org/

Educational Evaluators International
P.O. Box 5397
Los Alamitos, CA 90720
Tel: 562-431-2187, Fax: 562-943-5021
E-mail: Not Available
Web: Not Available

Educational International
29 Denton Road
Wellesley, MA 02181
Tel: 781-235-7425, Fax: Not Available
E-mail: Not Available
Web: Not Available

Educational Records Evaluation Services
777 Campus Commons Road, Suite 200
Sacramento, CA 95825
Tel: 916-565-7475, Fax: 916-565-7476
E-mail: edu@eres.com
Web: www.eres.com

Evaluation Service
P.O. Box 1455
Albany, NY 12201
Tel: 518-672-4522, Fax: Not Available
E-mail: esi@capital.net
Web: Not Available

International Consultants of Delaware
109 Barksdale Professional Center
Newark, DE 19711
Tel: 302-737-8715, Fax: 302-737-8756
E-mail: icd@icdel.com
Web: http://www.icdel.com

International Credentialing Associates
1 Progress Plaza, Ste. 810
St. Petersburg, FL 33701
Tel: 813-821-8852, Fax: Not Available
E-mail: Not Available
Web: Not Available

International Education Research Foundation
P.O. Box 66940
Los Angeles, CA 90066
Tel: 310-390-6276, Fax: 310-342-7086
E-mail: info@ierf.org
Web: http://www.ierf.org/

Joseph Silny & Associates International Education Consultants
P.O. Box 248233
Coral Gables, FL 33124
Tel: 305-666-0233, Fax: 305-666-4133
E-mail: info@jsilny.com
Web: http://www.jsilny.com/

The Knowledge Company
10301 Democracy Lane, Suite 403
Fairfax, VA 22030-2521
Tel: 703-359-3520, Fax: 703-359-3523
E-mail: tkco@knowledgecompany.com
Web: http://knowledgecompany.com/

Spantran Educational Services, Inc.
7211 Regency Square Blvd., Suite 205
Houston, TX 77036-3197
Tel: 713-266-8805, Fax: 713-789-6022
E-mail: info@spantran-edu.com
Web: http://www.spantran-edu.com/

Word Communication International
4501 N. 12th St.
Phoenix, AZ 85014
Tel: 602-265-0678, Fax: 602-265-2335
E-mail: evaluations@earthlink.com
Web: Not Available

World Education Services
P.O. Box 745
New York, NY 10113
Tel: 212-966-6311, Fax: 212-739-6100
E-mail: info@wes.org
Web: http://www.wes.org/

NOTE: ALWAYS CHECK WITH THE UNIVERSITY, ACADEMIC OR PROFESSIONAL BODY YOU ARE PREPARING THE CREDENTIAL REFORT FOR PRIOR TO SELECTING A PARTICULAR EVALUA-TION SERVICE TO BE CERTAIN THE SERVICE MEETS THEIR REQUIREMENTS.

Take responsibility for everything in your life.
Make yourself go beyond where you think you can go.

Teddy Atlas

Chapter III

Attending a Foreign
Accredited Law School

For those of you whose schedule and lifestyle permit, you may wish to attend as an internal law student at a foreign law school. Naturally, you will be competing for space with other students and some preference may be given to students who are citizens of the country where the school is located. By and large, however, admission is likely to be more liberal than with U.S. ABA law schools. Furthermore, many foreign law schools qualify for the U.S. Department of Education sponsored student loan program. This means that you may be eligible for deferred student loans for attending a foreign law school if you are a U.S. citizen or resident.

What Degree Will You Earn?

Upon successfully completing all academic requirements, the foreign university(s) will confer the LL.B. degree upon you. For those of you who are not familiar with this degree, let me assure you that the Juris Doctor (J.D.) degree is the academic equivalent of the LL.B. degree. In fact, don't take my word for it, the *American Heritage Dictionary;* Second College Edition defines Juris Doctor as "An academic degree that is the equivalent of a bachelor of laws." [That is, a LL.B.]

The United States is one of the only common law countries that confers the J.D. degree as a first law degree and, this is, historically speaking, a recent occurrence. Prior to the 1960s U.S. law schools also conferred the LL.B. degree upon their graduates. All other countries following the common law of England, (e.g., UK, Canada, Australia, and the current and former commonwealth nations) confer the LL.B. degree—the law degree meeting the legal education requirements for becoming a lawyer. To further illustrate this point, the law degree above the J.D. is the LL.M., or master of laws and the S.J.D., J.S.D., or LL.D. is the terminal degree in law, that is, the true "Doctor of Laws" degree.

Note, as of this writing, Australia, recently began offering the J.D. degree, but it is properly offered as an advanced law degree and not a first law degree. (See Appendix G)

> *"...your foreign legal education should be quite similar to what students of U.S. ABA approved law schools learn—in fact, it will be "substantially equivalent" to such education."*

What Type of Law Will I Learn at a Foreign Law School?

All of the law schools and programs listed in this book are situated in countries that follow the common law of England, which, of course, includes the United States. With this in mind, your foreign legal education should be quite similar to what students of U.S. ABA approved law schools learn—in fact, it will be "substantially equivalent" to such education. The core subjects will vary very little from country to country and the elective subjects are generally quite similar as well.

For example, in the United Kingdom all law students must meet the following core requirements before their legal education is deemed to qualify them for the practice of law. The core courses are known as the "Seven Foundations" and are listed below:

The Seven Foundations of Legal Knowledge

1) Obligations I: Contract
The foundations governing the enforceability of contracts, together with their performance and discharge, including the remedies available to parties and the doctrine of privity, and includes an outline of the law of restitution.

2)   Obligations II: Tort

The foundations of tortuous liability (including vicarious and joint liability) and remedies in respect of torts (including damages). There should be a sufficient study of the major torts (such as negligence, nuisance, intentional interference with the person and defamation) to exemplify the application of the general principles and the defenses, and to familiarize the student with the principle torts and their constituent elements.

3)   Criminal Law

The general foundations of criminal liability and a sufficient study of the major offenses (such as homicide, non-fatal offenses against the person and theft) to exemplify the application of the general principles and familiarize the student with the principle offenses and their constituent elements.

4)   Equity and the Law of Trusts

The relationship between Equity and Common Law. The trust as used for family or commercial or for public charitable purposes. Express, resulting and constructive trusts of property. Trustees' powers and obligations. Nature and scope of fiduciary obligations. Nature and scope of equitable rights and equitable remedies, especially tracing. Mareva injunctions, Anton Piller Orders, specific performance, imposition of personal liability to account as constructive trustee, estoppel entitlements to property or compensation, the developing principle of unconscionability.

5)   The Law of the European Union

The political institutions and processes of the European Communities. The European Court of Justice and its jurisdiction. Sources and general principles of the law of the European Union. The relationship between the law of the European Union and National Law. An introduction to the main areas of the substantial law of the European Union.

6)   Property Law

The foundation concepts of land law, the relationship between the common law and equitable rights, the scope, the nature and effect of estates and interest in land. An introduction to the strict settlement, trusts for sale and co-ownership and (in essentials) the relationship of landlord and tenant. An introduction to registered conveyancing.

7) Public Law

The basic features and characteristics of the constitution. Constitutional Law should cover the main institutions of government (Parliament, Executive and courts) in the United Kingdom and the European Union; civil liberties and the European Court of Human Rights; the sources of law and the law-making processes.

As you can see, with the exception of the requirement of European Union Law, the remaining core subjects may be found at almost any ABA-approved law school. Incidentally, European Union law is actually offered as an elective course at many ABA law schools. Also, don't be fooled into thinking that the UK law schools require only seven subjects—these are only core courses. Furthermore, when comparing the specific number of subjects required for graduation in a foreign law school verses U.S. law schools, remember that most foreign law schools offer full year courses rather than semesterized courses. For example, the typical contract course in ABA schools is broken down into semester courses (Contracts I, Contracts II, etc.) while a similar foreign law subject will cover the entire subject, but as a one-year course.

CASE STUDY

A close colleague of mine, Jerry B., is one of those people who just thrives on education. He has earned several degrees, and has always excelled in his military, banking, and economics career, but like most of you reading this book, Jerry always wanted to be a lawyer. Now Jerry is a bright guy, a very bright guy who could have easily been accepted to any law school, but he chose another path, he went to the UK to attend law school. Why? First of all, tuition fees were about one third of the cost of that of an ABA law school, but even more important, Jerry studied at one the most prestigious law schools in the world, Wolverhampton University. Now then, Wolverhamton did not attain such an elevated reputation by giving away law degrees, quite the contrary, law students enrolled in the law program must undergo a very rigorous schedule of study, much like that expected of ABA law school students. I know this was not an easy task and

Jerry has my highest respect for completing such a demanding degree.
Since graduating and entering the legal profession, Jerry has worked for several top international law firms. He became a well-respected international lawyer establishing his practice in the United States, England and the Caribbean. I can tell you that his legal expertise is just astounding. Jerry bypassed the traditional method of becoming a lawyer, but lost nothing in the process except, perhaps, $100,000 in student loans that he would still owe if he had gone to an ABA-approved law school. And, I know very few "traditionally" trained lawyers who can go toe-to-toe with Jerry inside or outside the courtroom.

Let's take a look at the foreign law schools that will accept foreign applicants:

List of Accredited Foreign Law Schools

Law Schools in the United Kingdom

The UK universities and colleges selected below offer law degrees recognized by the Law Society and the Bar Council as qualifying law degrees, that is, they meet the requirements for legal education for lawyers (solicitors or barristers). Further, many of these universities have registered with the U.S. Department of Education and have been approved under U.S. guaranteed student loan programs. If they have, you should be able to get a deferred student loan if you are accepted to that school. For your assistance I have indicated the Federal School Codes for those schools that currently have one. Since foreign schools are always making new applications for this status, be sure to check with the particular school(s) you have selected to see if they have recently been approved.

The following is a list of accredited law schools in the United Kingdom:

Anglia Law School
Victoria Road South,
Chelmsford Essex, CM1 1LL, England, UK
Tel: 01245 493131, Fax: 01245 493134
E-mail: s.s.byrne@apu.ac.uk
Web: http://www.anglia.ac.uk/law/chelmsford/llb.htm
Law Degrees Awarded:
     LLB - Law
     BA - Combined Honours

Birkbeck College School of Law, University of London
Malet Street, London
WC1E 7HX, England, UK
Tel: +44 (0) 20 7631 6507, Fax: +44 (0) 20 7631 6506
US Federal Student Loan School Code # G09084
E-mail: admin@law.bbk.ac.uk
Web: http://www.bbk.ac.uk/law/dept.htm
Law Degrees Awarded:
     LLB - Part-time

Birmingham University, Faculty of Law
Edgbaston, Birmingham B15 2TT, England, UK
Tel: +44 (0) 121 414 3637, Fax: +44 (0) 121 414 3585
U.S. Federal Student Loan School Code # G08908
E-mail: law@bham.ac.uk
Web: http://www.law.bham.ac.uk.htm
Law Degrees Awarded:
     LLB - Law
     LLB - Law with French
     LLB - Law & Business Studies
     LLB - Law & Politics
     LLB - Law & European Law

Bournemouth University School of Finance & Law
Poole, BH12 5BB, England, UK
Tel: +44 (0) 1202 595187, Fax: +44 (0) 1202 595261
E-mail: fandl@bournemouth.ac.uk
Web: http://www.bournemouth.ac.uk/fal.html
Law Degrees Awarded:
      LLB - Business Law (Sandwich)
      LLB - Law
      LLB - Law & Taxation
      LLB - Business Law (Sandwich)
      LLB - Law
      LLB - Law & Taxation

University of Brighton, Brighton Business School
Mithras House, Lewes Road
Brighton, East Sussex, BN2 4AT, England, UK
Tel: +44 1273 642987, Fax: +44 1273 642980
E-mail: bbsvwl@brighton.ac.uk/bbs
Web: http://www.bus.brighton.ac.uk/bbs/
Law Degrees Awarded:
      BA - Law with Accountancy

University of Bristol, Faculty of Law
Wills Memorial Building, Queens Road
Bristol BS8 1RJ, England, UK
Tel: +44 (0) 117 954 5329, Fax: +44 (0) 117 925 1870
U.S. Federal Student Loan School Code # G07632
E-mail: law-dept@bris.ac.uk
Web: http://www.law.bris.ac.uk.html
Law Degrees Awarded:
      LLB - Law
      LLB - Law & French
      LLB - Law & German
      LLB - European Legal Studies
      BSc - Chemistry and Law

Brunel University, Faculty of Law
Uxbridge, Middlesex, UB8 3PH, England, UK
Tel: +44 (0) 1895 274 000, Fax: +44 (0) 1895 232 806
E-mail: www@brunel.ac.uk
Web: http://www.brunel.ac.uk/
Law Degrees Awarded:
>LLB - Business & Finance Law
>LLB - Law
>LLB - French/German
>BSc - Economics & Law (incl. Sandwich)
>BSc - Management Studies & Law

University of Buckingham, Faculty of Law
Hunter Street
Buckingham, MK18 1EG, England, UK
Tel: +44 (0) 1280 814080, Fax: +44 (0) 1280 822245
E-mail: info@buckingham.ac.uk
Web: http://www.buckingham.ac.uk
Law Degrees Awarded:
>LLB - Part-time
>LLB - Law (2 years duration)
>LLB - European Studies (2 years duration)
>LLB - Law, Biology & Environment (2 years duration)
>LLB - Politics & Law (2 years duration)

Cambridge University, Faculty Board of Law
10 West Road
Cambridge CB3 9DZ, England, UK
Tel: +44 (0) 1223 330033, Fax: +44 (0) 1223 330055
U.S. Federal Student Loan School Code # G21777
E-mail: admin@law.cam.ac.uk
Web: http://www.law.cam.ac.uk/
Law Degrees Awarded:
>BA - Law Tripos

Cardiff University Law School
PO Box 427, Cardiff
CF10 3XJ, Wales, UK
Tel: +44 (0) 29 2087 4348, Fax: +44 (0) 29 2087 4097
E-mail: Law-UG@cardiff.ac.uk
Web: http://www.cf.ac.uk/claws.html
Law Degrees Awarded:
    LLB - Law
    LLB - Law & French
    LLB - Law & German
    LLB - Law & Italian
    LLB - Law & Japanese
    LLB - Law & Spanish
    LLB - Law & Sociology
    LLB - Law & Politics
    LLB - Law & Criminology

University of Central England in Birmingham
Birmingham, B42 2SU, England, UK
Tel: +44 (0) 121 331 6600, Fax: +44 (0) 121 331 6740
E-mail: postmaster@uce.ac.uk
Web: http://www.uce.ac.uk
Law Degrees Awarded:
    LLB - Part-time

City University, Faculty of Law
Northampton Square London EV1V 0HB, England, UK
Tel: +44 (0) 20 7040 8301, Fax: + 44 (0) 20 7040 8578
E-mail: law@city.ac.uk
Web: http://www.city.ac.uk/law/
Law Degrees Awarded:
    LLB - Law
    LLB - Business Law

Coventry University School of Law
Coventry, CV1 5FB, England, UK
Tel: +44 (0) 24 7688 8256, Fax: +44 (0) 24 7688 8679
U.S. Federal Student Loan School Code # G22571
E-mail: isladmin@coventry.ac.uk
Web: http://www.coventry-isl.org.uk.htm
Law Degrees Awarded:
    LLB - Part-time
    LLB - Legal Studies
    LLB - European Law with a Language
    LLB - Business Law
    LLB - Criminal Justice
    LLB - with English

De Montfort University School of Law
Elfed Thomas Building
Leicester, LE1 9BH, England, UK
Tel: +44 (0) 116 257 7177, Fax: +44 (0) 116 257 7186
E-mail: rwward@dmu.ac.uk
Web: http://www.dmu.ac.uk/Faculties/BL/law1.html
Law Degrees Awarded:
    LLB - Part-time
    LLB - Law
    LLB - Law with French
    LLB - Law with German
    BA   - Law
    BSc - Combined Studies (Qualifying Route Only)

University of Derby School of Law
Kedleston Road
Derby, DE22 1GB, England, UK
Tel: +44 (0) 1332 591446, Fax: +44 (0) 1332 622 736
E-mail: T.Wragg@derby.ac.uk
Web: http://www.derby.ac.uk/hll/law/lawnav.html
Law Degrees Awarded:
    LLB - Part-time
    LLB - Law

University of Dundee
Nethergate, Dundee DD1 4HN, Scotland, UK
Tel: +44 (0) 1382 34 4160, Fax: +44 (0) 1382 348 34 8150
E-mail: srs@dundee.ac.uk
Web: http://www.dundee.ac.uk/admissions/
Law Degrees Awarded:
      LLB - English Law
      LLB - Law & Accountancy
      LLB - Law with French
      LLB - Law with German

University of Durham, Department of Law
50 North Bailey
Durham DH1 3ET, England, UK
Tel: +44 (0) 191 374 2033, Fax: +44 (0) 191 374 2044
E-mail: Francis.Pritchard@durham.ac.uk
Web: http://www.dur.ac.uk/Law/
Law Degrees Awarded:
      LLB - Law
      BA   - Law & Economics
      BA   - Law & Politics
      BA   - Law & Sociology
      LLB - European Legal Studies

University of East Anglia, Faculty of Law: Norwich
NR4 7TJ, England, UK
Tel +44 (0) 1603-592520, Fax: +44 (0) 1603 250245
U.S. Federal Student Loan School Code # G10915
E-mail: law@uea.ac.uk
Web: http://www.ues.ac.uk/law/aboutlaw.htm
Law Degrees Awarded:
      LLB - Law
      LLB - Law with German Law & Language
      LLB - Law with French Law & Language
      LLB - Law with European Legal Systems
      LLB - Law with American Legal Studies

University of East London School of Law
Barking Campus, Longbridge Road
Essex RM8 2AS, England, UK
        Tel: +44 (0) 20 8223 2113, Fax: +44 (0) 20 8223 2927.
U.S. Federal Student Loan School Code # G30450
E-mail: p.berwick@uel.ac.uk
Web: http://www.uel.ac.uk/law/law_first-page.htm
Law Degrees Awarded:
        LLB - Part-time

University of Essex, Faculty of Law
Wivenhoe Park, Colchester, CO4 3SQ, England, UK
Tel: +44 (0) 1206 872 566, Fax: +44 (0) 1206 873 428
U.S. Federal Student Loan School Code # G08687
E-mail: law@essex.ac.uk
Web: http://www2.essex.ac.uk/law/
Law Degrees Awarded:
        LLB - Law
        LLB - English & European Laws
        LLB - English & French Law
        LLB - European Law with Sociology
        LLB - Law &European Studies
        LLB - Law & French
        LLB - Law & German
        LLB - Law & Russian
        LLB - Law & Philosophy
        LLB - English & French Law/ Maitrisse en Droit University
                of Paris X (Nanterre)
        LLB - Law & Human Rights
        LLB - Law & Politics

University of Exeter School of Law, Faculty of Law
Amory Building
Rennes Drive, Exeter,WX4 4RJ, England, UK
Tel: +44 (0) 1392 263371, Fax: +44 (0) 1392 263196
E-mail: S.O.Hammond@ex.ac.uk
Web: http://www.ex.ac.uk/law/
Law Degrees Awarded:
        LLB - Law
        LLB - European Law
        BA   - (Law) Law & Society
        BA   - (Law) Chemistry & Law

University of Glamorgan School of Law
Pontypridd, CF37 1DL, Wales, UK
Tel: +44 (0) 1443 480
E-mail: enquires@glam.ac.uk
Web: www.glam.ac.uk/law
Law Degrees Awarded:
      LLB - Part-time
      LLB - Law

University of Greenwich Law School
Bank House, Wellington Street
London, SE18 6PF, England, UK
Tel: +44 (0) 181 331 8590, Fax: Not Available
E-mail: courseinfo@gre.ac.uk
Web: http://www.gre.ac.uk/law/
Law Degrees Awarded:
      LLB - Law
      BA   - Law

University of Hertfordshire
College Late, Hatfield, Herts, AL10 9AB, England, UK
Tel: +44 (0) 1707 284800, Fax: +44 (0) 1707 284870
E-mail: Admissions@herts.ac.uk
Web: http://www.herts.ac.uk/law/
Law Degrees Awarded:
      LLB - Part-time
      LLB - Law
      LLB - Law (Accelerated Programme - 2 years duration)
      BSc - Combined Studies
      BA   - Social Science
      BA   - Business Studies (Law Major)

Huddersfield University, Department of Law
Queensgate, Huddersfield, HD1 3DH England, UK
Tel: +44 (0) 1484 422288, Fax: +44 (0) 1484 472753
E-mail: hubs@hud.ac.uk
Web: http://www.hud.ac.uk/schools/hubs/law/law.htm
Law Degrees Awarded:
      LLB - Part-time
      LLB - Law
      LLB - Business Law
      BA   - Law & Accountancy

The University of Hull Law School
Cottingham Road, HU6 7RX, England, UK
Tel: +44 (0) 1482 465857, Fax: +44 (0) 1482 466388
E-mail: law@hull.ac.uk
Web: http://www.law.hull.ac.uk.html
Law Degrees Awarded:
>LLB - Part-time
>LLB - Law
>LLB - Law with French
>LLB - Law with German
>LLB - Law & Sociology
>LLB - Law & Philosophy
>LLB - Law & Politics

Keele University, Faculty of Law
Staffordshire, ST5 5BG, England, UK
Tel:+44 (0) 1782 583 218, Fax: +44 (0) 1782 583 228
E-mail: law_office@keele.ac.uk
Web: http://www.keele.ac.uk/depts/la/home.htm
Law Degrees Awarded:
>BA - Law & Another Subject

Kent Law School, University of Kent
Canterbury, Kent, CT2 7NS, England, UK
Tel: +44 (0) 1227 827832, Fax: +44 (0) 1227 827831
U.S. Federal Student Loan School Code # G08665
E-mail: kls-webadmin@ukc.ac.uk
Web: http://www.ukc.ac.uk/law/
Law Degrees Awarded:
>LLB - Law
>LLB - English & French Law
>LLB - English & German Law
>LLB - English & Italian Law
>LLB - English & Spanish Law
>LLB - European Legal Studies
>BA - Combined Studies

King's College School of Law
University of London: Strand
London WC2R 2LS, England, UK
Tel: +44 (0) 20 7836 5454, Fax: +44 (0) 20 7848 2912
U.S. Federal Student Loan School Code # G09085
E-mail: enq.genlaw@klc.ac.uk
Web: http://www.klc.ac.uk/depsta/law/
Law Degrees Awarded:
      LLB - Law
      LLB - English & French Law
      LLB - Law with German Law
      LLB - European Legal Studies

Kingston School of Law
Kingston Hill, Kingston-upon-Thames
Surrey KT2 7LB, England, UK
Tel: +44 (0) 20 8547 2000, Fax: +44 (0) 20 8547 7038
E-mail: M.Beard@kingston.ac.uk
Web: http://law.kingston.ac.uk/
Law Degrees Awarded:
      LLB - Part-time
      LLB - Law
      LLB - Law with French
      LLB - Law with German
      BA   - Accounting & Law

Lancashire Law School
University of Central Lancashire
Preston PR1 2HE, England, UK
Tel: +44 (0) 1 772 893 062, Fax: +44 (0) 1 772 893 972
E-mail: lstudies@uclan.ac.uk
Web: http://www.uclan.ac.uk/facs/class/legalstu/
Law Degrees Awarded:
      LLB - Part-time
      LLB - Law
      LLB - Law & French
      LLB - Law & German
      BA   - Law (Combined Honours)
      BSc - Law (Combined Honours)

Lancaster University, Faculty of Law
Lancaster, LA1 4YN, England, UK
Tel: +44 (0) 1524 65201 ext. 2463, Fax: +44 (0) 1524 848137
U.S. Federal Student Loan School Code # G09444
E-mail: Law@Lancaster.ac.uk
Web: http://www.lancs.ac.uk/users/law/index.htm
Law Degrees Awarded:
      LLB - Law
      LLB - European Legal Studies

University of Leeds, Faculty of Law
20 Lyddon Terrace
Leeds, LS2 9JT, England, UK
Tel: +44 113 233 5033, Fax: +44 113 233 5056
E-mail: lawvis@leeds.ac.uk
Web: http://www.leeds.ac.uk/law/law.html
Law Degrees Awarded:
      LLB - Law
      LLB - English Law with a European Law
      LLB - Law & Chinese Studies
      LLB - Law & Japanese Studies
      LLB - Law & French Studies

Leeds Metropolitan University School of Law
Cavendish Hall
Beckett Park, Leeds, LS6 3QS England, UK
Tel: +44 (0) 113 283 7549, Fax: +44 (0) 113 283 3206
E-mail: international@lmu.ac.uk
Web: http://www.lmu.ac.uk/lbs/law/law.htm
Law Degrees Awarded:
      LLB - Part-time
      LLB - Law
      BA   - Law with Information Technology

University of Leicester School of Law
University Road
Leicester, LE1 7RH, England, UK
Tel: +44 (0) 116 252 2363, Fax: +44 (0) 116 252 5023
U.S. Federal Student Loan School Code # G22291
E-mail: Law@le.ac.uk
Web: http://www.le.ac.uk/la/ug/laug.html
Law Degrees Awarded:
> LLB - Law
> LLB - Law with French Law & Language
> LLB - Law European Union
> BA   - Economics and Law

University of Lincoln
Cottingham Road
Kingston upon Hull, HU6 7RT, England, UK
Tel: +44 (0) 1482 463671, Fax: +44 (0) 1482 463696
E-mail: international@lincoln.ac.uk
Web: http://www.ulh.ac.uk/law.html
Law Degrees Awarded:
> BA - Law & Another Subject

University of Liverpool School of Law
Liverpool L69 7ZS, England, UK
Tel: +44 (0) 151 794 2807, Fax: +44 (0) 151 794 2829
E-mail: law@liverpool.ac.uk
Web: http://www.liv.ac.uk/law/adm/degree.htm
Law Degrees Awarded:
> LLB - Law
> LLB - Law & French
> LLB - Law & German
> LLB - Law & Accounting
> LLB - Law & Economics

London School of Economics Law Department
University of London
P.O. Box 13401, Houghton Street
London WC2A 2AS, England, UK
Tel: +44 (0) 20 7955 7124/7125, Fax: +44 (0) 20 7955 6368
U.S. Federal Student Loan School Code # G06693
E-mail: ug-admissions@lse.ac.uk
Web: http://www.lse.ac
Law Degrees Awarded:
> LLB - Law
> LLB - Law with German
> LLB - Law with French
> LLB - Law & Anthropology
> LLB - Law & Government

London Guildhall University, Department of Law
84 Moorgate
London, EC2M 6SQ, England, UK
Tel: +44 (0) 20 7320 1500, Fax: +44 (0) 7320 1525
E-mail: Not Available
Web: http://www.lgu.ac.uk/law/side.htm
Law Degrees Awarded:
> LLB - Part-time
> LLB - Law
> LLB - Business Law
> BA   - Legal Studies
> BA   - Law and Another Discipline

University of Luton, Department of Law
Vicarage Street, Luton
LU1 3JU, England, UK
Tel: +44 (0) 1582 489030, Fax, +44 (0) 1582 743466
E-mail: law@luton.ac.uk
Web: http://www.luton.ac.uk/depts/law/courses.shtml
Law Degrees Awarded:
> LLB - Part-time

Manchester Metropolitan University School of Law
Hathersage Road
Manchester, M13 0JA, England, UK
Tel: +44 (0) 161 247 3049, Fax: +44 (0) 161 247 6309
U.S. Federal Student Loan School Code # G30333
E-mail: law.cse@mmu.ac.uk
Web: http://www.did.stu.mmu.ac.uk/depts/law/
Law Degrees Awarded:
      LLB - Law
      LLB - Part-time Evenings
      LLB - Law with French
      LLB - Law with German

Manchester University School of Law
Oxford Road
Manchester, M13 9PL, England, UK
Tel: +44 (0) 161 275 3560, Fax: +44 (0) 161 275 3579
U.S. Federal Student Loan School Code # G22797
E-mail: law_undergrad@man.ac.uk
Web: http://www.man.ac.uk/welcome/
Law Degrees Awarded:
      LLB - Law
      LLB - English & French Law
      BA   - Accounting & Law
      BA   - Government & Law

Middlesex University, Faculty of Law
The Burroughs, London, NW4 4BT, England, UK
Tel: +44 (0) 970 491 2305, Fax: +44 (0) 970 491 5501
E-mail: mdxna@aol.com
Web: http://mubs.mdx.ac.uk
Law Degrees Awarded:
      LLB - Law
      BA   - Law (Major)

Mid-Kent College
Horsted Centre, Maidstone Road
Chatham, Kent, ME5 9UQ, England, UK
Tel: +44 (0) 1634 830633, Fax: +44 (0) 1634 830224
E-mail: course.enquiries@midkent.ac.uk
Web: http://www.midkent.ac.uk
Law Degrees Awarded:
>BA - Law & Business Studies
>BA - Law & European Studies
>BA - Law & Politics
>BA - Law & Psychology
>BA - Law & Social Science

Newcastle Law School
Newcastle-upon-Tyne NE1 7RU, England, UK
Tel: +44 (0) 191 222 7624, Fax: +44 (0) 191 212 0064
E-mail: Newcastle.Law-School@ncl.ac.uk
Web: http://www.ncl.ac.uk/
Law Degrees Awarded:
>LLB - Law
>BA   - Accounting & Law
>BA   - Law with French

University of North London
266-220 Holloway Road
London, N7 6DB, England, UK
Tel: +44 (0) 20 7753 5169, Fax: +44 (0) 20 7753 5408
U.S. Federal Student Loan School Code # G22353
E-mail: international@unl.ac.uk
Web: http://www.unl.ac.uk
Law Degrees Awarded:
>LLB - Part-time
>LLB - Law

University of Northumbria School of law
Sutherland Building, Room 111
Newcastle Upon Tyne, NE1 8ST., England, UK
Tel: +44 (0) 191 227 4513, Fax: +44 (0) 191 227 4557
E-mail: la.information@unn.ac.uk
Web: http://law.unn.ac.uk/international.htm
Law Degrees Awarded:
>LLB - Part-time
>LLB - Law
>LLB - French & English Law

Nottingham Trent University Law School
Chaucer Building, Chaucer Street
Nottingham, NG1 4BU, England, UK
Tel: +44 (0) 115 8484270, Fax: +44 (0) 115 8486489
U.S. Federal Student Loan School Code # G30925
E-mail: Nicola.nightingale@ntu.ac.uk or alicecrofts@ntu.ac.uk
Web: http://www.nls.ntu.ac.uk/
Law Degrees Awarded:
 LLB - Part-time
 LLB - Law
 LLB - Law (Sandwich)
 LLB - Magisterial Law
 LLB - Europe with French
 LLB - Europe with German

University of Nottingham, Department of Law
University Park, Nottingham, NG7 2RD, England, UK
Tel: +44 (0) 115 951 6565, Fax: +44 (0) 115 951 6566
U.S. Federal Student Loan School Code # G08920
E-mail: undergraduate-enquiries@nottingham.ac.uk
Web: http://www.nottingham.ac.uk/
Law Degrees Awarded:
 LLB - Law
 BA - Law
 BA - Law & Politics
 BA - Law with American Law & Politics
 BA - Law & Chinese Law & Politics
 BA - Law with European Law & Politics
 LLB/BA - Law & South East Asian Law
 LLB/BA - Law & Chinese Law
 LLB/BA - Law with American Law
 LLB/BA - Law with European Law

School of Oriental and African Studies Department of Law
University of London
Thornhaugh Street, Russell Square
London, WC1H 0XG, England, UK
Tel: +44 (0) 20 7898 4670, Fax +44 (0) 20 7898 4669
E-mail: kd16@soas.ac.uk
Web: http://www.soas.ac.uk/Law/Home.html
Law Degrees Awarded:
 LLB - Law
 BA - Law & Another Discipline
 BA - Law & a Language

Oxford Brookes University
Headington, Oxford, OX3 0BP, England, UK
Tel: +44 (0) 1865 483750, Fax: +44 (0) 1865 483937
E-mail: sl@brookes.ac.uk
Web: http://www.brookes.ac.uk/schools/social/
Law Degrees Awarded:
LLB - Part-time
LLB - Law
BA - Law & Another Subject

University of Oxford, Faculty of Law
St. Cross Building, St. Cross Road
Oxford OX1 3UL, England, UK
Tel: +44 (0) 1865 2 71490, Fax: 44 (0) 1865 2 71493
U.S. Federal Student Loan School Code # G08394
E-mail: john.gardner@law.ox.ac.uk
Web: http://www.law.ox.ac.uk/
Law Degrees Awarded:
BA - Jurisprudence

University of Plymouth
Drake Circus, Plymouth, PL4 8AA, England, UK
Tel: +44 (0) 1752 600600, Fax: Not Available
E-mail: humanscience@plymouth.ac.uk
Web: http://www.plymouth.ac.uk
Law Degrees Awarded:
LLB - Law

University of Portsmouth
Milton Site, Locksway Road
Southsea, Hants, P.O.4 8JF, England, UK
Tel: +44 (0) 23 9284 8484   Fax: +44 (0) 23 9284 3082
E-mail: info.centre@port.ac.uk
Web: http://www.port.ac.uk
Law Degrees Awarded:
BA - Law & Accounting
BA - Law & Business
BA - Law & Human Resource Management
BA - Law & Languages

Queen Mary College
University of London
Mile End Road
London, E1 4NS, England, UK
Tel: +44 (0) 20 7882 3282, Fax: +44 (0) 20 8981 8733
U.S. Federal Student Loan School Code # G06697
E-mail: law-enquiries@qmul
Web: http://www.laws.qmw.ac.uk
Law Degrees Awarded:
      LLB - Law
      LLB - English & European Law
      LLB - Law with German Language
      BA   - Law & Economics
      BA   - Law & Politics
      BA   - Law & German

University of Reading, Department of Law
Whiteknights, P.O. Box 217, Reading, RG6 2AH, England, UK
Tel: +44 (0) 118 931 6568, Fax: +44 (0) 975 3280
U.S. Federal Student Loan School Code # G10143
E-mail: law@reading.ac.uk
Web: http://www.rdg.ac.uk./AcaDepts/lb/
Law Degrees Awarded:
      LLB - Law
      LLB - Law with French Law
      LLB - Law with Legal Studies in Europe

Sheffield Hallam University, Faculty of Law
Collegiate Crescent Campus
Sheffield, S10 2BP, England, UK
Tel: +44 (0) 114 225 2543, Fax: +44 (0) 114 225 2430
U.S. Federal Student Loan School Code # G30803
E-mail: sslenquiries@shu.ac.uk
Web: http://www.shu.ac.uk
Law Degrees Awarded:
      LLB - Part-time
      LLB - Law
      LLB - Law (Canada)
      LLB - Law (Maitress en Droit) Francais
      BA   - Law & Criminology

University of Sheffield, Department of Law
Crookesmoor Building, Conduit Road
Sheffield, S10 1FL, England, UK
Tel: +44 (0) 114 222 6771, Fax: +44 (0) 114 222 6832
U.S. Federal Student Loan School Code # G08398
E-mail: j.p.hill@sheffield.ac.uk
Web: http://www.shef.ac.uk/law/
Law Degrees Awarded:
      LLB - Law
      BA - Law
      BA - Law & Criminology
      BA - Law with French
      BA - Law with German
      BA - Law with Spanish

University of Southampton, Faculty of Law
Highfield, Southampton, SO17 1BJ, England, UK
Tel: +44 (0) 23 8059 2596, Fax: +44 23 8059 3024
E-mail: Undergrad.Law@soton.ac.uk
Web: http://www.soton.ac.uk/~law/
Law Degrees Awarded:
      LLB - Law
      BSc - Accounting & Law
      BSc - Politics & Law

Southampton Institute, The Law School
East Park Terrace, Southampton
Hampshire, SO14 0YN, England, UK
Tel: +44 (0) 1703 319000, Fax: +44 (0) 1703 235948
U.S. Federal Student Loan School Code # G08399
E-mail: si.law@solent.ac.uk
Web: http://www.solent.ac.uk/law/
Law Degrees Awarded:
      LLB - Law
      BA - Business & Law

Staffordshire University Law School
Leek Road, Stoke on Trent
Staffordshire, ST4 2DF, England, UK
Tel: +44 (0) 1782 294550, Fax: +44 (0) 1782 294335
E-mail: A.E.Holmes@staffs.ac.uk
Web: http://www.staffs.ac.uk/schools/law/
Law Degrees Awarded:
>LLB - Part-time
>LLB - Law
>LLB - Law & Language
>LLB - Law & Accounting
>BA - Modern Studies
>BA - Law & Another

University of Sunderland
St. Peter's Campus, St. Peter's Way
Sunderland SR6 0DD, England, UK
Tel: +44 (0) 191 515 2311, Fax: +44 (0) 191 515 2308
E-mail: international@sunderland.ac.uk
Web: http://my.sunderland.ac.uk/web/schools/
Law Degrees Awarded:
>LLB - Law
>LLB - Law & Business
>LLB - Law & Psychology
>LLB - Law & Philosophy
>BA - Law with Accounting (1999 Intake)
>BA - Law with Business

University of Surrey, Faculty of Law
Guildford, Surrey, GU2 7XH, England, UK
Tel: +44 (0) 1483 686200, Fax: +44 (0) 1483 686201
U.S. Federal Student Loan School Code # G09860
E-mail: information@surrey.ac.uk
Web: http://www.surrey.ac.uk/
Law Degrees Awarded:
>LLB - Law & European Studies
>LLB - Law & French
>LLB - Law & German
>LLB - Law & Russian
>BSc - French & Law
>BSc - German & Law
>BSc - Russian & Law

University of Sussex, School of Legal Studies
Arts C Building
Falmer, Brighton, BN1 9SN, England, UK
U.S. Federal Student Loan School Code # G06699
Tel: +44 (0) 1273 678562, Fax: +44 (0) 1273 678466
E-mail: wnquiries.sls@sussex.ac.uk
Web: http://www.sussex.ac.uk/
Law Degrees Awarded:
      LLB - Law
      LLB - European Commercial Law
      BA   - Law with North American Studies
      BA   - Law and Economics
      BA   - Law with History
      LLB/BA - Law with French
      LLB/BA - Law with German
      LLB/BA - Law with Italian
      LLB/BA - Law with Spanish
      LLB/BA - Law with Russian

Swansea Law School
Mount Pleasant, Swansea, SA1 6ED, England, UK.
Tel: +44 (0) 1792 481169, Fax: +44 (0) 1792 481169
E-mail: enquiry@sihe.ac.uk.
Web: http://www.sihe.ac.uk/faculty/humed/lawintro.htm
Law Degrees Awarded:
      LLB - Law

Thames Valley University
Ealing Campus, St. Mary's Road
Ealing, London, W5 5RF, England, UK
Tel: +44 (0) 20 8579 5000, Fax: +44 (0) 20 8566 1353
E-mail: learning.advice@tvu.ac.uk
Web: http://www.tvu.ac.uk/
Law Degrees Awarded:
      LLB - Part-time
      BA   - Criminal Justice Part-time

University of Teesside, Faculty of Law
Borough Road
Middlesborough, TS1 3BA, England, UK
Tel: +44 (0) 1642 384019, Fax: +44 (0) 1642 342399
E-mail: arts@tees.ac.uk
Web: http://www.tees.ac.uk/schools/socialsciences/law_content.cfm
Law Degrees Awarded:
    LLB - Law
    LLB - Part-time

University College London, Department of Law
Bentham House, Endsleigh Gardens
London, WC1H 0EG, England, UK
Tel: +44 (0) 20 7679 2000, Fax: Not Available
E-mail: Not Available
Web: http://www.ucl.ac.uk/laws/
Law Degrees Awarded:
    LLB - Law
    LLB - Law with Advanced Studies
    LLB - Law with French Law
    LLB - Law with German Law
    LLB - Law with Italian Law
    BA - Law & History

University College Northampton
Boughton Green Road
Northampton, NN2 7AL, England, UK
Tel: +44 (0) 1604 735500, Fax: +44 (0) 1604 721214
E-mail: international@northampton.ac.uk
Web: http://www.nene.ac.uk/
Law Degrees Awarded:
    LLB - Law

University of Wales, Aberystwyth, Department of Law
Hugh Owen Building, Penglais
Aberystwyth, Ceredigion, SY23 3DY, Wales, UK
Tel: +44 (0) 1970 622712, Fax: +44 (0) 1970 622729
      E-mail: daf@aber.ac.uk
Web: http://www.aber.ac.uk/law/
Law Degrees Awarded:
    LLB - Law

University of Wales, Swansea, Faculty of Law
Singleton Park, Swansea, SA2 8PP, Wales, UK
Tel: +44 (0) 1792 295831, Fax: +44 (0) 1792 295855
E-mail: laadmin@swan.ac.uk
Web: http://www.swan.ac.uk/law/
Law Degrees Awarded:
      LLB - Law
      LLB - Law with Business Studies, Language & Politics

University of Warwick School of Law
Coventry, Warwickshire, CV4 7AL, England, UK
Tel: +44(0) 24 7652 3075, Fax: +44 (0) 24 7652 4105
E-mail: Babara.Gray@warwick.ac.uk
Web: http://law.warwick.ac.uk/lawschool/
Law Degrees Awarded:
      LLB - Law
      LLB - European Law
      BA   - Law & Sociology
      BA   - Law & Business

University of the West of England, Faculty of Law
Frenchay Campus, Coldharbour Lane
Bristol, BS16 1QY, England, UK
Tel: +44 (0) 117 344 2604, Fax: +44 (0) 117 344 3368
U.S. Federal Student Loan School Code # G21948
E-mail: law@uwe.ac.uk
Web: http://www.uwe.ac.uk/law/default_ie.htm
Law Degrees Awarded:
      LLB - Part-time

University of Westminster School of Legal Studies
4-12 Little Titchfield Street
London, W1W 7UW, England, UK
Tel: +44 (0) 20 7911 5000, Fax: Not Available
E-mail: k.mcphee@wmin.ac.ul
Web: http://www.wmin.ac.uk/law
Law Degrees Awarded:
      LLB - Part-time

Wolverhampton University, School of Legal Studies
Molineux Street
Wolverhampton, England, WV1 1SB UK
Tel: +44 (0) 1902 321058, Fax: +44 (0) 1902 322696
U.S. Federal Student Loan School Code # G30851
E-mail: a.baily@wlv.ac.uk
Web: http://www.wlv.ac.uk/sls/school/school.html
Law Degrees Awarded:
      LLB - Law
      BA   - Law (Major)
      LLB - Part-time

LAW SCHOOLS IN NORTHERN IRELAND – UK

Queens University, Belfast, Faculty of Law
28 University Square
Belfast, BT7 1NN Northern Ireland, UK
Tel: +44 (0) 28 9027 3451, Fax: +44 (0) 28 9027 3376
U.S. Federal Student Loan School Code # G22736
E-mail: law-enquiries@qub.ac.uk
Web: http://www.law.qub.ac.uk
Law Degrees Awarded:
      LLB - Law
      LLB - Law & Accounting
      LLB - Common & Civil Law with French
      BSc - Legal Science Degree

University of Ulster
Shore Road, Newtownabbey, Co.
Antrim, BT37 0QB, Northern Ireland, UK
Tel: +44 (0) 8 700 400 700, Fax: Not Available
E-mail: online@ulst.ac.uk
Web: http://www.ulst.ac.uk
Law Degrees Awarded:
      BA - Government & Law
      BA - Law & Economics

LAW SCHOOLS IN IRELAND

The Honourable Society of the Kings Inns
Henrietta Street Dublin 1, Ireland
Tel: 353 1 874 4840 Fax: 353 1 872 6048
E-mail: info@kingsinns.ie
Web: http://www.kingsinns.ie/html/home.html
Law Degrees Awarded:
    Diploma in Legal Studies
    Degree of Barrister-at-Law

The Incorporated Law Society of Ireland
Blackhall Place Dublin 7, Ireland
Tel: 353 1 672 4802 Fax: 353 1 672 4992
E-mail: lawschool@lawsociety.ie
Web: http://www.lawsociety.ie/educ.htm
Law Degrees Awarded:
    Diploma in Property Tax
    Diploma in Applied European Law
    Diploma in Legal French and the Certificate in Legal German
    Diploma in Commercial Law
    Diploma in E-Commerce
    Diploma in Applied Finance

Trinity College Faculty of Law
Dublin 2, Ireland
Tel: 353 1 677 2941 Fax: 353 1 671 0037
 E-mail: secretary@tcd.ie
Web: http://www.tcd.ie
Law Degrees Awarded:
    LLB - Law

University College Cork, Faculty of Law
County Cork, Ireland
Tel: 353 21 490 3249 Fax: 353 21 490 3413
U.S. Federal Student Loan School Code # G06704
E-mail: lawfac@ucc.ie
Web: www.ucc.ie/ucc/depts/law
Law Degrees Awarded:
    BCL - Law
    BCL - French/German

University College Dublin, Faculty of Law
Belfield, Dublin 4, Ireland
Tel: 353 1 706 1425   Fax: 353 1 706 1070
U.S. Federal Student Loan School Code # G10188
E-mail: admissions@ucd.ie
Web: http://www.ucd.ie/
Law Degrees Awarded:
      BCL - Law

University College Galway Faculty of Law
Galway, County Galway, Ireland
Tel: 353 91 750348 Fax: 353 91 750506
E-mail: law.faculty@nuigalway.ie
Web: www.nuigalway.ie/law
Law Degrees Awarded:
      LLB - Law

University of Limerick Law Department
Limerick, Ireland
Tel: 353 61 202344 Fax: 353 61 202682
U.S. Federal Student Loan School Code # G30843
E-mail: Raymond.friel@ul.ie
Web: www.ul.ie/~law
Law Degrees Awarded:
      LLB - Law
      LLB - 2 year

LAW SCHOOLS IN AUSTRALIA

Australia National University, Faculty of Law
Fellows Road
Canberra, ACT 2601, Australia
Tel: +61 2 6125 3483, Fax: Not Available
E-mail: enquiries.law@anu.edu.au
Web: http://law.anu.edu.au/index.asp
Law Degrees Awarded:
      LLB - Law
      LLB - Law & Actuarial Studies
      LLB - Law & Commerce
      LLB - Law & Psychology
      LLB - Law & Science

Bond University School of Law
Gold Coast, Queensland 4229, Australia
Tel. +61 7 5595 2011, Fax. +61 7 5595 2246
E-mail: law@bond.edu.au
Web: http://www.bond.edu.au/law/
Law Degrees Awarded:
> LLB - Law
> LLB - Honours
> LLB - Business
> LLB - Jurisprudence

James Cook University, Faculty of Law
Townsville, Queensland 4811, Australia
Tel: +61 7 4781 4111, Fax: +61 7 4779 6371
U.S. Federal Student Loan School Code # G12206
E-mail: InternationalStudentCentre@jcu.edu.au
Web: www.jcu.edu.au
Law Degrees Awarded:
> LLB - Law
> LLB - Law & Business
> LLB - Law & Economics
> LLB - Law & Public Policy

Deakin University
Waurn Ponds, Geelong, Victoria 3217, Australia
Tel: +61 3 5227 1091, Fax: +61 3 5227 2286
E-mail: jnorton@deakin.edu.au
Web: www.law.deakin.edu.au
Law Degrees Awarded:
> LLB - Law
> LLB - Law & Commerce
> LLB - Law & International Studies

Flinders University, Faculty of Law
Sturt Road
Bedford Park, South Australia 5042, Australia.
Tel: +61 8 8201 2727, Fax: +61 8 8201 3177
U.S. Federal Student Loan School Code # G11091
E-mail: Intl.Office@flinders.edu.au
Web: http://www.flinders.edu.au/
Law Degrees Awarded:
> LLB - Laws
> LLB - Honours

Griffith University, Faculty of Law
Messines Ridge Road
Mt. Gravatt, Queensland 4122, Australia
Tel: +61 7 3875 5339, Fax: +61 7 3875 5599
E-mail: guic@mailbox.gu.edu.au
Web: http://www.gu.edu.au/
Law Degrees Awarded:
    LLB - Law

La Trobe University
Bundoora, Victoria 3083, Australia
Tel: +61 3 9479 1199, Fax: +61 3 9479 3660
U.S. Federal Student Loan School Code # G30961
E-mail: international@latrobe.edu.au
Web: http://www.latrobe.edu.au/
Law Degrees Awarded:
    LLB - Law

Macquarie University School of Law
Balaclava Road
North Ryde, Sydney, New South Wales 2113, Australia
Tel: +61 2 9850 7314, Fax: Not Available
E-mail: iso@mq.edu.au
Web: http://www.mq.edu.au/
Law Degrees Awarded:
    LLB - Law
    LLB - Law (Distance Learning)

Monash University School of Law
Wellington Road Clayton
Victoria 3168, Australia
Tel: +61 3 9627 4852, Fax: +61 3 9627 4862
E-mail: monashdirect@adm.monash.edu.au
Web: http://www.monash.edu.au/
Law Degrees Awarded:
    LLB - Law
    LLB - Law & Business
    LLB - Law & Finance
    LLB - Law & Economics
    LLB - Law & Commerce
    LLB - Law & Education

Murdoch University, Law Faculty
South Street Murdoch
Western Australia 6150, Australia
Tel: +61 8 9360 6977, Fax: Not Available
U.S. Federal Student Loan School Code # G25796
E-mail: kphutch@central.murdoch.edu.au
Web: http://www.murdoch.edu.au/
Law Degrees Awarded:
    LLB - Law

Newcastle University, Department of Legal Studies
University Drive Callaghan,
New South Wales 2308, Australia
Tel: +61 2 4921 6595, Fax: +61 2 49601 766
U.S. Federal Student Loan School Code # G26232
E-mail: international-admissions@newcastle.edu.au
Web: http://www.newcastle.edu.au/
Law Degrees Awarded:
    LLB - Law
    LLB - Law & Business
    LLB - Law & Finance
    LLB - Law & Economics
    LLB - Law & Science

Queensland University of Technology School of Law
Gardens Point, Queensland 4000, Australia
Tel: +61 7 3864 3142, Fax: +61 7 3864 3529
E-mail: qut.international@qut.edu.au
Web: http://www.qut.edu.au/
Law Degrees Awarded:
    LLB - Law
    LLB - Law & Business
    LLB - Law & Finance
    LLB - Law & Economics
    LLB - Law & Journalism

University of Adelaide School of Law
North Terrace Adelaide
South Australia 5000, Australia
Tel: +61 8 8303 5063, Fax: +61 8 8303 4344
U.S. Federal Student Loan School Code # G31000
E-mail: law@adelaide.edu.au
Web: http://www.law.adelaide.edu.au/
Law Degrees Awarded:
> LLB - Law
> LLB - Law & Business
> LLB - Law & Finance
> LLB - Law & Economics
> LLB - Engineering

University of Canberra School of Law
Kirinari Street Bruce
ACT 2617, Australia.
Tel: +61 (02) 6201 5762, Fax: +61 (02) 6201 5764
U.S. Federal Student Loan School Code # G30915
E-mail: dmtlaw@management.canberra.edu.au
Web: http://www.dmt.canberra.edu.au/law/
Law Degrees Awarded:
> LLB - Law

University of Melbourne School of Law
Parkville, Victoria 3052, Australia
Tel: +61-3-8344-4000, Fax: +61-3-8344-5104
E-mail: post@law.unimelb.edu.au
Web: http://www.law.unimelb.edu.au/
Law Degrees Awarded:
> LLB - Law
> LLB - Law Honours
> LLB - Law & Business
> LLB - Law & Finance
> LLB - Law & Economics
> LLB - Engineering
> LLB - Arts

University of New England, Faculty of Law
Armidale, New South Wales 2351, Australia
Tel: +61 2 6773 3333, Fax: +61 2 6773 3122
E-mail: admissions@metz.une.edu.au
Web: http://www.une.edu.au/
Law Degrees Awarded:
    LLB - Law
    LLB - Law & Business
    LLB - Law & Finance
    LLB - Law & Economics
    LLB - Law (Distance Learning)

University of New South Wales School of Law
Sydney, New South Wales 2052, Australia
Tel: +61 2 9385 2227, Fax: +61 2 9385 1175
E-mail: law@unsw.edu.au
Web: http://www.law.unsw.edu.au/
Law Degrees Awarded:
    LLB - Law
    LLB - International Studies
    LLB - Business
    LLB - Jurisprudence
    LLB - Languages

University of Queensland, Faculty of Law
St. Lucia, Queensland 4072, Australia
Tel: + 61 (7) 3365 9017, Fax: + 61 (7) 3365 4788
E-mail: facbel@bel.uq.edu.au
Web: http://www.uq.edu.au/bel/
Law Degrees Awarded:
    LLB - Law

University of Sydney, Faculty of Law
173 Phillip Street, Sidney
New South Wales 2000, Australia
Tel: +61 2 9351 0351 Fax: +61 2 9351 0200
U.S. Federal Student Loan School Code # G30672
E-mail: info@law.usyd.edu.au
Web: http://www.law.usyd.edu.au/
Law Degrees Awarded:
    LLB - Law & Joint Degrees

University of Tasmania, Faculty of Law
Churchill Avenue Sandy Bay
Tasmania 7001, Australia
Tel: +61 3 6226 2999 Fax: +61 3 6226 2087
E-mail: Not Available
Web: http://info.utas.edu.au
Law Degrees Awarded:
    LLB - Law

University of Western Australia Law School
Mounts Bay Road Crawley
Western Australia 6000, Australia
Tel: +61 2 9380 3792, Fax: Not Available
E-mail: mschneider@ecel.uwa.edu.au
Web: www.law.ecel.uwa.edu.au/law
Law Degrees Awarded:
    LLB - Law

University of Western Sydney, Faculty of Law
P.O. Box 1000
St. Mary's, New South Wales 2760, Australia
Tel: +61 2 9685 9626, Fax: +61 2 9685 9625
E-mail: f.nkala@usw.edu.au
Web: http://www.uws.edu.au/law
Law Degrees Awarded:
    LLB - Law
    LLB - Law & Business
    LLB - Law & Finance
    LLB - Law & Economics
    LLB - Engineering
    LLB - Arts

University of Wollongong, Faculty of Law
Northfields Avenue Wollongong
New South Wales 2522, Australia
Tel: +61 2 4221 3555 Fax: +61 2 4221 3233
U.S. Federal Student Loan School Code # G30914
E-mail: uniadvice@uow.edu.au
Web: http://www.uow.edu.au/
Law Degrees Awarded:
     LLB - Law
     LLB - Law & Business
     LLB - Law & Finance
     LLB - Law & Economics
     LLB - Computer Science
     LLB - Arts

LAW SCHOOLS IN NEW ZEALAND

Auckland University, Faculty of Law
9 Eden Crescent
Auckland 1, New Zealand
Tel: +64 9 373-7599, Fax: +64 9 373-7440
U.S. Federal Student Loan School Code # G12421
E-mail: postmaster@auckland.ac.nz or international@auckland.ac.nz
Web: http://www.law.auckland.ac.nz/
Law Degrees Awarded:
     LLB - Law
     LLB - Law Honours
     LLB - Law & Commerce
     LLB - Law & Finance
     LLB - Law & Health Science
     LLB - Law & Property

University of Canterbury, Faculty of Law
Private Bag 4800
Christchurch 1, New Zealand
Tel: +64 3 366 7001, Fax: +64 3 364 2999
U.S. Federal Student Loan School Code # G22253
E-mail: admissions@laws.canterbury.ac.nz
Web: http://www.laws.canterbury.ac.nz/
Law Degrees Awarded:
     LLB - Law

University of Otago Faculty of Law
P.O. Box 56
Dunedin, New Zealand
Tel: +64 3 479 8857, Fax: +64 3 479 8855
E-mail: law@otago.ac.nz
Web: http://www.otago.ac.nz/law
Law Degrees Awarded:
 LLB - Law

University of Waikato School of Law
Private Bag 3105
Hamilton, New Zealand
Tel: +64 7 838 4167, Fax: +64 7 838 4417
E-mail: law@waikato.ac.nz
Web: http://www.waikato.ac.nz/law/homepage.html
Law Degrees Awarded:
 LLB - Law
 LLB - Law & Management
 LLB - Law And Science

Victoria University of Wellington Faculty of Law
P.O. Box 600
Wellington, New Zealand
Tel: +64 4 463 5350, Fax: +64 4 463 5056
U.S. Federal Student Loan School Code # G12078
E-mail: International-Students@vuw.ac.nz
Web: http://www.vuw.ac.nz/
Law Degrees Awarded:
 LLB - Law
 LLB - Law Honours
 LLB - Conjoint Degree

LAW SCHOOLS IN HONG KONG

City University of Hong Kong, Department of Law
83 Tat Chee Avenue
Kowloon Tong, Kowloon, Hong Kong
Tel: 852 2788 7365, Fax: 852 2788 7363
E-mail: lwgo@cityu.edu.hk
Web: http://www.cityu.edu.hk/slw/
Law Degrees Awarded:
 LLB - Law Honours

University of Hong Kong, Department of Law
Room 604, KK Leung Bldg
Pokfulam Road, Hong Kong
Tel: 852 2859 2111, Fax: 852 2558 2549
E-mail: lawfac@hkusua.hku.hk
Web: http://www.hku.hk/
Law Degrees Awarded:
    LLB - Law

LAW SCHOOLS IN SINGAPORE

National University of Singapore Faculty of Law
10 Kent Ridge Crescent
Singapore 119260
Tel: 6 775 6666, Fax: 6 779 0979
E-mail: enquire@nus.edu.sg
Web: http://www.nus.edu.sg/
Law Degrees Awarded:
    LLB - Law

LAW SCHOOLS IN THE CARIBBEAN

Barbados
University of the West Indies Faculty of Law
Cave Hill Campus
P.O. Box 64
Bridgetown, Barbados
Tel: 246 417 4215, Fax: 264 242 1788
E-mail: aburgess@uwichill.edu.bb
Web: http://law.uwichill.edu.bb/
Law Degrees Awarded:
    LLB - Law

Cayman Islands
Cayman Islands Law School (Administered by Liverpool Law School, UK)
Tower Building
P.O. Box 495
Grand Cayman, Cayman Islands
Tel: +44 (0) 151 794 2807, Fax: +44 (0) 151 794 2829
E-mail: law@liverpool.ac.uk
Web: http://www.liv.ac.uk/law/cils/cils.htm
Law Degrees Awarded:
    LLB - Law

CANADIAN LAW SCHOOLS

Alberta
University of Alberta, Faculty of Law
4th Floor, Law Centre
Corner of 111th Street & 88th Avenue
Edmonton, Alberta T6G 2H5, Canada
Tel: 403-492-3115, Fax: 403-492-4924
E-mail: kjwilson@law.ualberta.ca
Web: http://www.law.ualberta.ca/
Law Degrees Awarded:
    LLB - Law

University of Calgary, Faculty of Law
2500 University Drive, N.W.
Calgary, Alberta T2N 1N4, Canada
Tel: 403-220-8154, Fax: 403-282-8325
E-mail: law@ucalgary.ca
Web: http://www.ucalgary.ca/
Law Degrees Awarded:
    LLB - Law

British Columbia
University of British Columbia, Faculty of Law
1822 East Mall
Vancouver, British Columbia V6T 1Z1, Canada
Tel: 604-822-3151, Fax: 604-822-8108
U.S. Federal Student Loan School Code # G08369
E-mail: borthwick@law.ubc.ca
Web: http://www.law.ubc.ca/
Law Degrees Awarded:
    LLB - Law

University of Victoria, Faculty of Law
P.O. Box 2400
Victoria, British Columbia V8W 3H7, Canada
Tel: 250-721-8150, Fax: 250-721-6390
U.S. Federal Student Loan School Code # G08370
E-mail: kclamp@uvvm.uvic.ca
Web: http://www.law.uvic.ca/
Law Degrees Awarded:
    LLB - Law

Manitoba
University of Manitoba, Faculty of Law
Robson Hall
Winnipeg, Manitoba R3T 2N2, Canada
Tel: 204-474-6130, Fax: 204-275-5540
U.S. Federal Student Loan School Code # G06684
E-mail: Not Available
Web: http://www.umanitoba.ca/Law/
Law Degrees Awarded:
      LLB - Law

New Brunswick
University of New Brunswick, Faculty of Law
P.O. Box 4400
Fredericton, New Brunswick E3B 5A3, Canada
Tel: 506-453-4669, Fax: 506-453-4604
E-mail: Not Available
Web: http://www.unb.ca/
Law Degrees Awarded:
      LLB - Law

University de Moncton, cole de droit
New Brunswick, E1A 3E9, Canada
Tel: 506-858-4560, Fax: 506-858-4534
E-mail: leblans@umoncton.ca
Web: http://www.umoncton.ca/
Law Degrees Awarded:
      LLB BCL - Law

Nova Scotia
Dalhousie Law School
6061 University Avenue
Halifax, Nova Scotia B3H 4H9, Canada
Tel: 902-494-2114, Fax: 902-494-1316
E-mail: LAWINFO@dal.ca
Web: http://as01.ucis.dal.ca/law/index.cfm
Law Degrees Awarded:
      LLB - Law

Ontario
Carleton University, Department of Law
Colonel By Drive
Ottawa, Ontario K1S 5B6, Canada
Tel: 613-520-3690, Fax: 613-520-4467
E-mail: law@carleton.ca
Web: http://www.carleton.ca/law/index.html
Law Degrees Awarded:
    LLB - Law

Osgoode Hall Law School
York University
4700 Keele Street
North York, Ontario M3J 1P3 Canada
Tel: 416-736-5712, Fax: Not Available
E-mail: admissions@osgoode.yorku.ca
Web: http://www.osgoode.yorku.ca/
Law Degrees Awarded:
    LLB - Law

Queens University, Faculty of Law
Kingston Ontario K7L 3N6, Canada
Tel: 613-533-2220, Fax: 613-533-6661
E-mail: olsas@ouac.on.ca
Web: www.queensu.ca/info
Law Degrees Awarded:
    LLB - Law

University of Ottawa, Faculty of Law
Louis Pasteur Fauteux Hall
Ottawa, Ontario K1N 6N5, Canada
Tel: 613-562-5794, Fax: 613-562-5124
E-mail: comlaw@uottowa.ca
Web: http://www.uottawa.ca/academic/commonlaw/
Law Degrees Awarded:
    LLB - Law

University of Toronto, Faculty of Law
78 Queen's Park
Toronto, Ontario M5S 2C5, Canada
Tel: 416-978-3716, Fax: Not Available
U.S. Federal Student Loan School Code # G06688
E-mail: law.admissions@utoronto.ca.
Web: http://www.utoronto.ca/
Law Degrees Awarded:
    LLB - Law
    JD - Law

University of Windsor, Faculty of Law
401 Sunset Avenue
Windsor, Ontario N9B 3P4, Canada
Tel: 519-253-3000 (ext. 2925), Fax: 519-973-7064
U.S. Federal Student Loan School Code # G06689
E-mail: UWLaw@uwindsor.ca
Web: http://cronus.uwindsor.ca/law
Law Degrees Awarded:
    LLB/JD - Law

Quebec
Laval University, Faculty of Law
Cite Universitaire Pavillon
Charles-de-Koninck Sainte-Foy, Quebec, G1K 7P4, Canada
Tel: 418-656-3036, Fax: 418-656-7230
E-mail: Not Available
Web: http://www.ulaval.ca/fd/
Law Degrees Awarded:
    BCL - Law

McGill University
3644 Peel Street, Room 15
Montreal, Quebec, H3A 1W9, Canada
Tel: 514-398-6604, Fax: 514-398-4659
U.S. Federal Student Loan School Code # G06677
E-mail: undergradadmissions.law@mcgill.ca
Web: http://www.law.mcgill.ca/
Law Degrees Awarded:
    BCL/LLB - Law

University de Montreal, Faculty of Law
C.P. 6128, Succ. Centre-Ville Montreal
Montreal H3C 3J7, Canada
Tel: 514-343-6124, Fax: 514-343-2199
E-mail: monique.laforest@umontreal.ca
Web: http://www.droit.umontreal.ca/
Law Degrees Awarded:
    BCL - Law

University de Quebec, Department of Law
455 Renz Levesque Blvd.
East Montreal, Quebec H2L 4Y2, Canada
Tel: 514-987-7096, Fax: 514-987-4784
E-mail: aecsd@er.uqam.ca
Web: http://www.juris.uqam.ca/
Law Degrees Awarded:
    BCL - Law

University of Sherbrooke
2500 University Blvd.
Sherbrooke, Quebec J1K 2R1, Canada
Tel: 819-821-7000, Fax: 819-821-7578
E-mail: information@courrier.usherb.ca
Web: http://www.usherbrooke.ca/
Law Degrees Awarded:
    BCL - Law

Saskatchewan
University of Saskatchewan, College of Law
Saskatoon, Saskatchewan, S7N 0W0, Canada
Tel: 306-966-5869, Fax: 306-966-5900
U.S. Federal Student Loan School Code # G22192
E-mail: beth.bilson@usask.ca.
Web: http://www.usask.ca/law/
Law Degrees Awarded:
    LLB - Law

LAW SCHOOLS IN SOUTH AFRICA

University of South Africa, Faculty of Law
P.O. Box 392
Pretoria 0001, South Africa
Tel: 27 12 429-3111
E-mail: hardic@unisa.ac.za
Web: http://www.unisa.ac.za/faculty/law/
Law Degrees Awarded:
> LLB - Law
> LLB - Law (Distance Learning)

Inside of a ring or out, ain't nothing wrong with going down. It's staying down that's wrong.

Muhammad Ali

Chapter IV

Earning a Foreign Accredited Law Degree by Distance Learning

Study Law Abroad Without Ever Leaving Your Home

There are a number of accredited foreign law schools that offer law degrees by distance learning. While studying law at a distance may seem unusual and, perhaps, a bit unorthodox, it is fairly normal in many countries. Remember, it is the knowledge of law that is important to the practitioner, not how he or she acquired that knowledge. As I pointed out earlier, this was once the way most lawyers studied law in the United States. There has even been a recent recognition of external law study by the ABA which has acquiesced to several external LL.M law-degree programs. In fact, ABA rules currently permit up to 12 credits by distance learning, video, audio, and Interment based chat rooms.

But don't expect that the ABA-approved law schools will open their arms and doors to this "new concept" overnight. There are just too many economic and political forces against distance learning. Even with the advent of the Internet, the wheels of progress in this regard turn very slowly—very slowly. But there is no need to wait for the system to change when you can be in the mainstream of legal education and earn your foreign law degree without ever leaving your armchair.

Moreover, you'll find that foreign distance-learning law programs are offered by schools that are not only fully accredited, but are also among the most prestigious law schools in the world. In addition to being able to obtain an outstanding and respected legal education, the study of law by distance learning offers many advantages, as follows:

- You can study law without ever leaving your home
- You can study law from your office, library or most anywhere
- You can study completely online
- You can study by correspondence (without a computer)
- You can take your examinations almost anywhere in the world
- Law books and study materials are delivered to your front door
- You can network with other students online or by correspondence
- You can save thousands of dollars over the cost of traditional legal education

And these are only a few of the many advantages of earning a law degree by distance learning, I'm sure you can think of many more. For now let's get started by looking at some of the more popular programs offered.

> *"Remember, it is the knowledge of law that is important to the practitioner, not how he or she acquired that knowledge."*

The British Distance Learning Law Schools

Four highly respected universities in the United Kingdom have programs that work quite well for American students and for students throughout the world. The University of London, Northumbria University, Nottingham-Trent University, and the University of Wolverhampton all have high-quality programs with no residency requirements and provide for examinations in all 50 states and countries throughout the world. Contact details are listed below:

Holborn College / University of Huddersfield"
Woolwich Road
Charlton, London SE7 8LN
United Kingdom
Tel: +44 (0) 20 8317 6000, Fax: +44 (0) 20 8317 6001
Email: flenq@holborncollege.ac.uk
Web: www.holborncollege.ac.uk
Law Degrees Awarded:
    LLB - (by distance learning)

The University of Huddersfield, in partnership with Holborn College, will begin a new distance-learning LLB degree program in August 2004. The University of Huddersfield is a well respected and dynamic institution with an excellent graduate employment record. The program offers three convenient start dates; September, January and May and, students without a bachelor degree may be eligible to enroll under the Mature Entry provisions if over 21 and have formal work experience.

University of London External Programme
Room 3, Senate House
Malet Street
London, WC1E 7HU, England, UK
Tel: +44 (0) 20 7862 8386, Fax: +44 (0) 20 7862 8383
E-mail: laws@external.lon.ac.uk
Web: www.londonexternal.ac.uk
Law Degrees Awarded:
    LLB - (by distance learning)

The University of London was founded in 1836 and is one of the oldest universities in the world, with an international reputation for excellence in the field of law. The university has been offering law degrees by distance learning to candidates around the world through the External Program since its inception.

The admission requirements for the law degree generally require one of the following:

- Bachelor's Degree from an accredited university or college or;
- Completion of A and O levels (required of UK and commonwealth applicants only)
- Some allowance may be made for "mature" students for career/academic experience.

After meeting the general admission requirements, completing the application and paying the applicable fees you will be offered a place as a registered law student. You will <u>not</u> need to take the LSAT and a low GPA should not preclude your admission.

The University of London statutes state that there is one standard for the LL.B. degree regardless of the mode of study the student chooses. This means that as an external student you will be held to the same rigorous standard as the law students sitting in the hallowed academic halls in London. As such, you may expect to experience the most intellectually challenging three or four years of your life. But if you persevere and work hard you will walk away with a legal education and law degree respected the world over.

University of Northumbria School of Law
Sutherland Building, Room 111
Newcastle Upon Tyne, NE1 8ST., England, UK
Tel: +44 (0) 191 227 4513, Fax: +44 (0) 191 227 4557
E-mail: la.information@unn.ac.uk
Web: http://law.unn.ac.uk/international.htm
Law Degrees Awarded:
    LLB - (by distance learning)

Northumbria University is located in Central Newcastle and boasts one on the most innovative distance-learning law programs in the world. In fact, the Quality Assurance Agency for Higher Education (QAA) rates Northumbria among the top law schools in the UK. The LL.B. Honours degree may be earned in four years entirely by distance learning. Students who already possess a bachelor's degree may complete the degree in three years. Furthermore, the four-year program has no formal entry requirements. This means that the university will admit students without a prior degree providing they demonstrate a "high level of motivation, discipline and the necessary intellectual ability required to complete a degree level course successfully." Students may demonstrate this by work experience or formal academic qualifications.

Northumbria also offers an optional two-week residency for distance learning students and students are permitted to transfer from distance learning to attendance at the university should the student desire to do so. As with all the British distance-learning law schools, there is no LSAT requirement.

Nottingham Trent University Law School
Chaucer Building, Chaucer Street
Notingham, NG1 4BU, England, UK
Tel: +44 (0) 115 8484270, Fax: +44 (0) 115 8486489

E-mail: Nicola.nightingale@ntu.ac.uk or alicecrofts@ntu.ac.uk
Web: http://www.nls.ntu.ac.uk/
Law Degrees Awarded:
    LLB - (by distance learning)

Nottingham Trent is a well known and respected university with a highly regarded LL.B program. The distance-learning program is relatively new, but I have heard good reports about it and it will likely become one of the more popular distance-learning programs around. The program offers distance learning with a personal touch. You will have access to personal advisors to help you through your three to four years of study, and the price is remarkably reasonable. The school is eager to enroll international students and will consider mature applicants over 21 years of age with suitable academic or career experience.

Wolverhampton University, School of Legal Studies
Molineux Street
Wolverhampton, England, WV1 1SB UK
Tel: +44 (0) 1902 321058, Fax: +44 (0) 1902 322696
E-mail: B.M.Mitchell2@wlv.ac.uk
Web: http://www.wlv.ac.uk/sls/
Law Degrees Awarded:
    LLB - Law (by distance learning)

Wolverhampton University has not been in existence as long as the University of London, however, it enjoys the same accreditation status. Wolverhampton operates under a Royal Charter, that is, by an Act of Parliament. The university was founded in 1974 and has rapidly become an innovator and leader in the study of law. The distance-learning program is highly respected and operates on the semester system that makes it more familiar and, to some extent, more practical for American students. The primary difference between the two universities is that the University of Wolverhampton breaks down the learning programs into three semesters per year with a final examination at the end of each semester. The University of London has only one academic period extending from October to May with final exams at the end of that period. One additional feature of the Wolverhampton program deserves mentioning. In Wolverhampton if you fail a particular subject, you can simply retake the examination for that subject in the next semester. The University of London is not so flexible; if you fail one subject you must repeat the entire year—including the subjects you passed—something to think about.

The Australian Distance Learning Law Schools

Macquarie University School of Law
Balaclava Road, North Ryde
Sydney, New South Wales 2113, Australia
Tel: +61 2 9850 7314, Fax: Not Available
E-mail: iso@mq.edu.au
Web: http://www.mq.edu.au/
Law Degrees Awarded:
      LLB - Law (by distance learning)

University of New England, Faculty of Law
Armidale, New South Wales 2351, Australia
Tel: +61 2 6773 3333, Fax: +61 2 6773 3122
E-mail: admissions@metz.une.edu.au
Web: http://www.une.edu.au/
Law Degrees Awarded:
      LLB - Law (by distance learning)

South Africa's Distance Learning Law School

University of South Africa, Faculty of Law
P.O. Box 392
Pretoria 0001, South Africa.
Tel: 27 12 429-3111, Fax: Not Available
E-mail: hardic@unisa.ac.za
Web: http://www.unisa.ac.za/faculty/law/
Law Degrees Awarded:
      LLB - Law (by distance learning)

Will Study by Distance Learning at the Universities be Difficult?

The study of law in any setting is extremely difficult. The foreign universities offering distance learning will provide you with some guidance and lists of suggested books and reading material, however, it is not likely that this material alone will insure your success. The truth of the matter is that more than 70% of the students who study alone will fail. For this reason a number of academic tutorial colleges offer assistance to bridge the gap for distance students to help overcome these abysmal statistics. Students who avail themselves of these academic services have a much higher pass rate—**about a 70% pass rate**. Why aren't the pass rates higher? Hey, this is law school, its not designed to be easy—but a 70% pass rate means you can make it to your goal—with the help of a good tutorial service.

> *"The truth of the matter is that more than 70% of the students who study alone will fail."*

Should you decide to pursue earning an accredited foreign-law degree by distance learning, I highly recommend you consider one of the tutorial programs listed below. Think about it, you have a 70% chance of passing if you use one of these services and a 70% chance of failing if you do not. True, you might be one of the exceptional people who can go it alone, but it's not likely. Don't fight the numbers. My advice is to get all the help that's available. The costs are generally very reasonable. In fact the total tuition fees for the British distance-learning law school and the cost of a good tutorial college combined will only run approximately $5,000.00 to $10,000.00 per year. That's quite a savings over the cost of most traditional American and Canadian law schools.

CASE STUDY

Take the example of another lawyer, Charlie S. Charlie earned his law degree externally from one of the most prestigious law schools in the world, the University of London External Programme. (See Chapter IV). This was no easy task and took a lot of dedication and hard work. Charlie had to go through an intense—and I mean *really* intense—four-year study program. Let me explain this, the University of London's program is one of the most difficult law-degree programs in the world, but it is also among the most respected. You see, the final examinations he took were the same as those taken by the university's internal students and they were graded by the same professors. I know for a fact that Charlie sweated out many intense moments waiting for his examination results, but one thing he didn't have to worry about was quitting his job or rushing to get to class—he studied externally, that is, by distance learning. But he did not have to study alone, he was able to network with other law students throughout the world. And his total cost for the degree probably averaged less than $5,000 per year. That's quite a bargain!

After completing his first law degree, Charlie elected to go on and earn an LL.M (Master of Laws degree) to increase his career options and marketability. Think about this, in the same time it took other law students to earn a J.D. the traditional way, Charlie earned two prestigious law degrees and, at a fraction of the cost of traditional legal education. Eventually, he took and passed the bar exam where he lived in California and is currently practicing law there. Dreams can become reality.

Tutorial Services Offering Programs For British Law Distance-Learning Students

United States

Crown Law Centre
380 Mountain Rd., Suite 1605
Union City, NJ 08087
Tel: 917-817-7688
E-mail: rivpowery@aol.com
Web: www.CrownLawCentre.com

Crown Law Centre offers a classroom law study program that includes cross registration with the University of London or Wolverhampton University. The program consists of weekly evening lectures in New York City. The school is directed by Prof. Rivington Powery, a personal friend and gifted teacher. If you live in the New York metropolitan area and want to experience traditional classroom study, you will not be disappointed.

International Center for Legal Studies
3227 Brownes Creek Road
Charlotte, NC 28269
Tel: 704-509-6711

E-mail: info@legaltutors.com
Web: www.legaltutors.com

The International Center for Legal Studies (ICLS) offers online law lectures to give students the classroom experience without leaving their home or office. Check their website for a sample demonstration of their unique e-learning system. The director, George Pappas, is a personal friend, attorney and gifted educator. ICLS offers an outstanding program that is perfect for distance learning students.

United Kingdom

ILEX Tutorial College
College House, Kempston
Bedford MK42 7AB UK
Tel: +44 01234 841010
E-mail: itslaw@ilex-tutorial.ac.uk
Web: www.ilex-turorial.ac.uk

Law Tutors Online
Tel: +44 020 8689 7734
E-mail: LTO@lawtutorsonline.co.uk
Web: www.lawtutorsonline.co.uk

Law Tutors Online is a web-based tutorial service designed to assist University of London distance-learning students in the study of law. An excellent feature is that LTO offers one-on-one personal tutoring for enrolled students.

Semple Piggot Rochez is a pioneer in web-based tutorial service designed to assist University of London distance-learning students in the study of law.

London Law Tutors
P.O. Box 10241
London SW19 8ZH, UK
+44 (0) 20 8453 7900
E-mail: llb@londlaw.demon.co.uk
Web: www.londlaw.demon.co.uk

What you know is more important than where or how you learned it.

Dr. Preston E. Pierce

Chapter V

American Distance Learning
Law Schools

California Distance Learning Law Schools

Most U.S. law schools are ABA-approved law schools. This, of course, means that some U.S. law schools are not ABA approved. For our purposes we are concerned only with those non-ABA law schools whose graduates are permitted to sit for the bar examination. Most of these schools require that you attend classes, a small number, however, offer law study by distance learning leading to the Juris Doctor (J.D.) degree.

The State of California has the unique distinction of being the only jurisdiction in the United States that permits graduates of California State Bar registered distance-learning law schools to sit for its bar examination. Technically speaking, these schools are not approved or accredited in the traditional manner; rather they are registered with the State Bar of California. What this means, for our purposes, is that graduates of these programs are conferred with the J.D. degree, but more importantly they may sit for the bar exam in California. Incidentally, even the ABA recently recognized, at least in part, the efficacy of distance learning. Currently ABA rules permit up to 12 credits by distance learning.

Now if you live in California you may be thinking this is a very viable alternative to the traditional path to becoming a lawyer—and you would, of course, be right. However, if you do not reside in California you may be thinking why in the world would I want to be a California attorney if I don't live there? Good question. The answer is that once you are admitted to practice in one state, other states may consider you as a qualified candidate to take their bar exam. (See more about this in Chapter VIII)

California law schools are being examined separately here because they offer the most in alternative approaches to the study of law leading to admittance to the Bar, but there are opportunities in other states as well which we will discuss later in this chapter.

Regardless of whether you choose to attend classes at an unaccredited California law school or to pursue your legal study through a California correspondence law school you must understand that despite the liberal school admissions' policies, you will have to work very hard or you simply will not make it. As with the accredited foreign law-school approach, admission to the program is relatively liberal, graduating is quite another story. I'm not trying to discourage you; I just don't want you to think that "alternative" means watered down, it surely is not.

General Admission Requirements for California Distance Learning Law Schools

Naturally, you will want to check with the schools directly for any specific admission requirements as they may change from time to time. However, the following is a list of the general admission requirements for most programs.

Before beginning the study of law, the candidate must have satisfied the Following:

Completed at least <u>two years of college</u> work, which college work shall be not less than one-half of the collegiate work acceptable for a bachelor's degree granted upon the basis of a four-year period of study by a college or university approved by the examining committee.

OR

Have attained in apparent intellectual ability the equivalent of at least two years of college work by taking examinations. For example, CLEP and other standardized examinations. (See **www.MaxStudy.com**)

Also, if the student ultimately plans to take the bar examination, they must register with the examining committee as a law student within 90 days after beginning the study of law. Naturally, some schools may impose higher admission requirements. The correspondence schools, for the most part, will require that you meet these minimum standards only. Why? Again, the answer boils down to economics: with the correspondence law schools you will not be competing for desk space.

First Year Law Students Examination: The Baby Bar

Okay, now you know the good part; it's easy to get into one of these California law schools. Now for the bad news, if you successfully complete your first year of study at a California unaccredited law school (by correspondence or attendance) you must demonstrate your mastery of the first years subjects by taking the First Year Law Students' Exam (FYLSX) "affectionately" referred to as the Baby Bar Exam.

> *"I am of the opinion that most nontraditional students just do not fully appreciate what they're up against."*

The baby bar exam will test your knowledge in the subjects of criminal law, contract law, and tort law. The test is given each year during the third week of June and October in California. The one-day exam consists of three essays, each of which must be completed in 52 minutes and 100 multiple-choice questions. The average pass rate over the past five years has been a little over 20%—not impressive. There has been much speculation as to why the pas rates are so low for the baby bar exam. There are two leading viewpoints on this issue:

(1)   Students just don't give the exam the respect it deserves and fail to properly prepare for it or,

(2)   The examination is designed to be unreasonably difficult to serve as a barrier for nontraditionally educated prospective lawyers.

Certainly both theories have some merit, however, I am of the opinion that most nontraditional students just do not fully appreciate what they're up against. True the exam is designed to be difficult, but not to be a barrier, rather it is designed to weed out those not prepared or not suited to the profession. The fact is that not everyone can or should be a lawyer. Better to find this out early before you waste your time, money, and effort in a field that is just not right for you. However, as with the strategies discussed for accredited foreign law schools, a cottage industry of legal tutorial services has developed to help increase the odds of passing in your favor. (See list of services at the end of this chapter.)

What happens if you don't pass the Baby Bar?

In the past failing the baby bar meant that your law studies would come to a halt unless and until you successfully passed it. Fortunately, under a new law, Section 6060(g) of the <u>California Business and Professionals Code</u>, students may continue their legal studies while waiting to take the examination. Section 6060(g) states, "those who pass the examination within the first three consecutive administrations . . . shall receive credit for all law studies completed at the time the examination is passed. . . ." However, you must take and pass the baby bar within three consecutive attempts after first becoming eligible to take it if you wish to receive credit for two years of law study. This means that you can take the exam up to the end of your sophomore year in law school without any loss of credit.

If you work hard and have what it takes, you can pass the baby bar exam—and ultimately the bar exam, but you will need some help. Most of the California correspondence law schools offer you little more than a potential opportunity to become a lawyer. Even the unaccredited California (attendance) law schools are generally more limited in what they offer students than the traditional ABA law schools. To bridge this gap you will need to consider using one of the tutorial law services that specialize in this area. I used America's Bar Review and passed on my first attempt. Again, a list of such services is available at the end of this chapter.

CASE STUDY

Take Steve K. for example. Steve started out working in a law office as a private investigator and legal assistant for a Southern law firm. Steve worked hard at raising a family and establishing himself as an invaluable employee, but Steve wanted more, he wanted to go to law school. He wanted to be a lawyer. Problem was that Steve did not live near a law school and, even if he did, he couldn't just quit his job and put his family in hock to pay off $80,000+ in student loans.

Fortunately, for Steve, there was a good solution. Steve learned that he could enroll in a California correspondence law school, Saratoga University, my *alma mater*. He studied diligently and received academic and practical assistance from the partners at the firm where he worked. For Steve this was a great advantage and worked even better than an ordinary lawyer apprenticeship program. (See Chapter VII) After several years he was awarded the J.D. degree. He immediately applied and was admitted to an LL.M program at an ABA law school (See Chapter VIII).

Steve recently finished his advanced law degree with distinction and he will be now be taking the next bar exam—way to go Steve!

Before we look at the law schools offering distance-learning programs, I want to again caution you that you will need some supplemental support from a baby bar preparation Service. Why? Law school is designed to teach you law, not to pass bar exams (including the baby bar exam). Let me give you a quick example of what I mean. I studied U.S. law at Saratoga University School of Law. I had a thorough and demanding syllabus and received academic support (that's important). But taking a bar exam is not what law school can or should prepare you for. Law school is about learning the law and learning to think in a lawyer-like manner. The bar examiners who write the baby bar and general bar examinations have a different job; they have to cull the flock a bit. Now don't get me wrong, you need a solid foundation of legal academics, but to pass the baby bar or general bar you need to learn some gamesmanship as well.

There are many good programs out there to help you in this respect, but three that stand out in my mind as being the best are:

(In alphabetical order)

Baby Bar Review Programs

America's Guaranteed Bar Review
725 J Street
Sacramento, CA 95814
Tel: 800-359-8010
Web: http://www.americaslegalbookstore.com/babybar.asp

Richard and Marie Finely have been in the business of helping law students to pass exams longer than anyone I know. They will take you in and treat you like one of their "kids" whether you're 23 or 73—I mean it! The program offers a comprehensive review for both the baby bar and the general bar exam in their spacious Sacramento classrooms or by home study. They also have a huge selection of nearly every law book ever written and they ship within 24 hours. I personally buy all my law books from them. They are my good friends—they're great!

Fleming's Fundamentals of Law
23166 Los Alisos Blvd.
Suite 238
Mission Viejo, CA 92691-2843
Tel: 949-770-7030
Web: http://www.lawprepare.com/

Fleming's has a great program and offers outlines and cassette tapes to help prepare you for the baby bar exam and the general bar exam as well. The tapes and written material are chock full of mnemonic devices and other aids to help you nail down the examination.

PasstheBar.com
12 25th Avenue # 3
Venice, CA 90291
Tel: 310-699-6891
Web: www.passthebar.com

Scott Pierce has been a legal-writing instructor for over 20 years. His credentials are impeccable and he covers all facets of bar-exam preparation, but specializes in teaching how to master the hardest part of any bar exam—the essays! If you need help in this area, Scott Pierce is without parallel.

Now, we're ready to take a look at the distance learning law degree programs.

U.S. Distance Learning Law Degree Programs

U.S. Distance Learning Law Degree Programs

Abraham Lincoln University
Suite 420, Fourth Floor
3000 South Robertson Boulevard
Los Angeles, CA 90034
Tel: 310-204-0222, Fax: 310-204-7025
E-mail: info@alu.edu
Web: http://www.alulaw.com/
Degrees Offered:
    Juris Doctor

British-American University School of Law
2026 Summer Wind
Santa Ana, CA 92704
Tel: (888) 264-3261, Fax: Not Available
E-mail: info@british-american.edu
Web: http://www.british-american.edu
Degrees Offered:
    Juris Doctor

Note: Jean Sasser, the Chancellor, is a friendly and well informed educator. British-American has risen in a few short years to become one of the elite distance-learning law schools. Also, Dr. Roger Agajanian, the school's founder, was a pioneer in bringing distance-learning legal education into the modern age. British-American was the first correspondence law school to offer online and interactive programs. (And, Roger and Jean are personal friends).

West Coast School of Law
7837 Danvers Street
Downey, CA 90240
Tel: 562-927-2330, Fax: Not Available
E-mail: info@ccls.info
Web: www.ccls.info
Degrees Offered:
　　Juris Doctor

West Coast School of Law has a terrific Dean, Dave Stallings, who understands what it is to be a distance-learning law student—he was one! West Coast is also boasts the lowest tuition of all the California Bar registered law schools. True price is not everything, but West Coast has so much to offer at such an affordable price you really have to at least consider them before you make a final choice. Dave is also a personal friend of mine.

Concord University School of Law
1133 Westwood Blvd., Suite 2000
Los Angeles, CA 90024
Tel: 800-439-4794, Fax: 888-564-6745
E-mail: infoconcord@concordlawschool.com
Web: www.ConcordLink.com
Degrees Offered:
　　Juris Doctor

Note: As with British-American, Concord runs an outstanding program with online teaching and interactive studies.

University of Honolulu School of Law
1031 McHenry Ave, Suite 13
Modesto, CA 95350
Tel: (209) 577-3161
Degrees Offered:
　　Juris Doctor

Newport University School of Law
20101 Southwest Birch, Suite 120
Newport Beach, CA 92660
Tel: 949-757-1155, Fax: 949-757-1156
E-mail: Not Available
Web: http://www.newport.edu
Degrees Offered:
> Juris Doctor

Northwestern California University School of Law
1750 Howe Avenue, Suite 535
Sacramento, CA 95825
Tel: 916-922-9303, Fax: 916-487-5681
E-mail: inquiry@nwculaw.edu
Web: http://www.nwculaw.edu
Degrees Offered:
> Juris Doctor

Oak Brook College of Law
P.O. Box 26870
Fresno, CA 93729
Tel: 559-650-7755, Fax: 559-650-7750
E-mail: info@obcl.edu
Web: http://www.obcl.edu/
Degrees Offered:
> Juris Doctor

Saratoga University School of Law
780 Blairwood Court
San Jose, CA 95120
Tel: 800-870-4246, Fax: Not Available
E-mail: mhn@saratoga.edu
Web: http://www.saratogau.edu/
Degrees Offered:
> Juris Doctor

Southern California University for Professional Studies College of Law
1840 East 17th Street #240
Santa Ana, CA 92705-8605
Tel: 800-477-2254, Fax: 714-480-0800
E-mail: info@scups.edu
Web: http://www.scups.edu
Degrees Offered:
> Juris Doctor

West Haven University Law Studies Program
6101 Ball Road
Cypress, CA 90630
Tel: 714-220-0782, Fax: 714-220-9726
E-mail: info@westhavenuniv.edu
Web: http://www.westhavenuniv.edu
Degrees Offered:
    Juris Doctor

William Howard Taft University
201 East Sandpointe Avenue
Santa Ana, CA 92707-5703
Tel: 800-882-4555 or 714-850-4800, Fax: 714-708-2082
E-mail: admissions@taftu.edu
Web: http://www.taftu.edu/
Degrees Offered:
    Juris Doctor

Taft is also an excellent school. They have been around and have passed the test of time. I hear only good things from Taft students and graduates.

Your chances of success in any undertaking can always be measured by your belief in yourself.

Robert Collier

Chapter VI

Attending American Unaccredited and State Approved Law Schools

Breaking the Code

This is a good time to discuss the confusing accreditation terminology that is often applied to non-ABA approved law schools. There are essentially three classifications used to label non-ABA schools. Let's take them in descending order according to their perceived level of credibility

State Approved/Accredited Law Schools

As discussed in Chapter II, the American Bar Association acts in an advisory capacity with respect to establishing the individual state requirements for admission to practice law. Obviously, one primary piece of "advice" is that only graduates of ABA-approved law schools should be permitted to practice law. Fortunately, this advice is merely advisory and not in any way mandatory. The states have the absolute right to establish their own rules of practice and many states, in fact, vigorously exercise this authority by providing for non-ABA law school graduates to be admitted to practice law in their jurisdiction.

All of the states listed in this chapter have established what are known as state-approved law schools. These schools are given a status almost equal to that of an ABA-approved school with respect to granting law graduates the right to sit for the bar examination in that particular state. Often, other states will also permit graduates of state-approved law schools to sit for the bar exam in their state notwithstanding that their law degree was not earned from an ABA law school. In this regard, state-approved law schools are nearly on an equal footing with ABA law schools, and many state-approved law schools are recognized as offering outstanding legal education, for example, Massachusetts School of Law at Andover or Humphreys College of Law in Stockton California. These are but a few of the many excellent state-approved/accredited law schools.

Unaccredited Law Schools

The next tier of non-ABA law schools is the unaccredited law schools. Although this term is used somewhat generically, even by this author, for clarification, the term is used here to describe those law schools that are not state approved, but are nonetheless granted the recognition and privilege of permitting their graduates to sit for the bar exam in that state. The primary difference between state-approved law schools and unaccredited law schools is that graduates of the former are often permitted to sit for the bar exam in a number of states, whereas graduates of the latter may normally only take the bar exam in the particular state in which the school is located.

For purposes of this chapter, the unaccredited law schools whose graduates may sit for the bar examination are located in the state of California only.

Bar Registered Correspondence and Distance-Learning Law Schools

Bar registered correspondence law schools are schools that are also unique to the state of California and are discussed in greater detail in the previous chapter. They are discussed here to help your understanding and to avoid the confusion caused by the misuse and misunderstanding of these terms. California is, of course, the only state that permits correspondence law study leading to a Juris Doctor degree. More importantly, it is the only state that will permit such graduates to sit for the general bar exam, assuming, of course that they have previously passed the baby bar examination. (See Chapter V).

For whatever peculiar reason, these correspondence schools are not granted the title of "unaccredited" but rather relegated to the lesser classification of "registered." Not to worry, for our purposes, graduates of all three tiers may sit for the bar examination in at least the state in which the school operates. Moreover, once you are admitted in one state you may apply for admission to practice or sit for the bar exam in a variety of other states. (See Chapter VIII)

> *"Now then, aside from the fact that you are attending a law school that is not ABA approved, your experience will be strikingly similar to traditional law schools."*

What To Expect From Classroom Attendance

Now then, aside from the fact that you are attending a law school that is not ABA approved, your experience will be strikingly similar to traditional law schools. You will be expected to study diligently, prepare for and attend classes regularly and to pass final examinations. As with ABA law schools, you will be in a highly competitive environment and all but the most serious players are washed out by the end of the first year. For example, Lincoln Law School in Sacramento California, welcomes its fledgling class of first year students with this warning, "take a look to the person to the right and left of you... you will not likely be seeing them next semester."

CASE STUDY

Another case is that of Warren W., an American who went to law school while in the military in the Philippines. Note that I do not list any Philippines law schools in this book because the Philippines is not a purely common-law country. Law in the Philippines is primarily what is known as civil law, but with just a hint of common law (a remnant of U.S. colonial law, I suppose). Still, there are many states that will permit such law graduates and practitioners to sit for their bar examination, subject to some conditions.

After leaving the military, Warren remained in the Philippines and practiced law for eight years. He eventually came back the United States, but was unaware that he was eligible to practice law here. He eventually became a Certified Public Accountant and enjoyed his work, but had never really quite accepted the fact that he was not a lawyer, at least in the U.S. Warren's love of the law eventually led him back to law school where I met him while studying for an LL.M in taxation. Warren knows tax law better than anyone I have ever met, but without a license to practice law, his talents would always remain somewhat limited despite the fact that he was a CPA.

Well, I happen to like and respect Warren a great deal so I couldn't just let him go on without letting him know what he's been missing all these years. I shared with Warren the very strategies you are now learning in this book and he was shocked that no one ever told him this before. But he really shouldn't have been surprised at all because these secrets are well guarded and only a very few know all the alternatives—including the staff at many state bar offices. Now, at the tender age of 50, he is preparing for the bar exam. You're never too old to realize your dream, In fact, Warren is actually a lot younger than other people I have counseled, the oldest was 70 years—young!

Join A Study Group

Regardless of how you choose to study law you are well advised to join a study group of law students. If you cannot find an existing group, start one yourself. When I was preparing for my juris doctorate degree from Saratoga University School of Law and the University of London, I quickly learned that it is nearly impossible to go it alone. When I was studying for my LL.M from an ABA law school, St. Thomas University, I thought I had evolved academically to a point where I no longer needed to work with a study group. I soon learned the folly of this attitude when halfway into the first semester I was getting desperate for help in understanding new and complex concepts in tax law. Fortunately I formed a study group with a group of some sharp and dedicated students and practitioners—I could not have made it without the support of my study group.

Whether you are studying in a classroom, by correspondence or online, most schools will connect you with other students and professors who want to network and form a study group. I cannot emphasize enough the value of being able to engage in intellectual discourse with your peers and professors. The study of law can be, as you will see, overwhelming at times. The support you get from such a group can make the difference between failure and success in law school. Take my advice on this one.

> *"Regardless of how you choose to study law you are well advised to join a study group of law students."*

State Bar Accredited/Approved Law School

Following is a list of state approved or accredited law schools that require classroom attendance:

Alabama

Birmingham School of Law
205 20th Street North
823 Frank Nelson Building
Birmingham, AL 35203
Tel: 205-322-6122, Fax: 205-322-2822
E-mail: admissions@bsol.com
Web: www.bsol.com
Degrees Offered:
        Juris Doctor

Miles Law School
5500 Myron Massey Boulevard
Birmingham, AL 35064
Tel: 205-929-1504, Fax: 205-923-7749
Email: Milelaw1@Bellsouth.net
Web: www.mlaw.edu/
Degrees Offered:
        Juris Doctor

Thomas Goode Jones School of Law
Montgomery, Alabama 36109-3398
Tel: 800-879-9816, Fax: Not Available
E-mail: amatthews@faulkner.edu
Web: www.faulkner.edu/jonesschooloflaw/welcome/default.cfm
Degrees Offered:
        Juris Doctor

California

Cal Northern School of Law
1395 Ridgewood Drive
Chico, CA 95973
Tel: 530-891-6900, Fax: Not Available
E-mail: info@calnorthern.edu
Web: www.calnorthern.edu
Degrees Offered:
Juris Doctor

Empire College School of Law
3035 Cleveland Ave.
Santa Rosa, CA 95403
Tel: 707-546-4000, Fax: 707-546-4058
E-mail: info@empcol.com
Web: www.empcol.com
Degrees Offered:
Juris Doctor

Glendale University College of Law
220 North Glendale Avenue
Glendale, CA 91206
Tel: 818-247-0770, Fax: 818-247-0872
E-mail: admissions@glendalelaw.edu
Web: www.glendalelaw.edu
Degrees Offered:
Juris Doctor

Humphreys College of Law
6650 Inglewood Avenue
Stockton, CA 95207
Tel: 209-478-0800, Ext: 116
Email: admissions@humphreys.edu
Web: www.humphreys.edu/law
Degrees Offered:
Juris Doctor

John F. Kennedy University School of Law
547 Ignacio Valley Road
Walnut Creek, CA 94596
Tel: 925-295-1800, Fax: Not Available
E-mail: law@jfku.edu
Web: www.jfku.edu/law
Degrees Offered:
Juris Doctor

Lincoln Law School of Sacramento
3140 "J" Street
Sacramento, CA 95816
Tel: 916-446-1275, Fax: 916-446-5641
E-mail: information@lincolnlaw.edu
Web: www.lincolnlaw.edu

Degrees Offered:
Juris Doctor

Lincoln Law School of San Jose
One North First Street
San Jose, CA 95113
Tel: 408-977-7227, Fax: Not Available
E-mail: deanlincoln@earthlink.net
Web: www.lincolnlawsj.edu
Degrees Offered:
Juris Doctor

Monterey College of Law
404 West Franklin Street
Monterey, CA 93940
Tel: 831-373-3301, Fax: 831-373-0143
E-mail: info@montereylaw.edu
Web: www.montereylaw.edu
Degrees Offered:
Juris Doctor

New College of California School of Law
50 Fell Street
San Francisco, CA 94102
Tel: 415-241-1302, Fax: 415-241-1353
E-mail: admissions@newcollege.edu
Web: www.newcollege.edu
Degrees Offered:
Juris Doctor

San Fernando Valley College of Law
21300 Oxnard Street
Woodland Hills, CA 91367
Tel: 818-883-0529, Fax: Not Available
E-mail: lfreeman@uwla.edu
Web: www.sfvlaw.edu
Degrees Offered:
    Juris Doctor

San Francisco Law School
20 Haight Street
San Francisco, CA 94102
Tel: 415-626-5550, Fax: 415-626-5584
E-mail: admin@sfls.edu
Web: www.sfls.edu
Degrees Offered:
    Juris Doctor

San Joaquin College of Law
901 5th Street
Clovis, CA 93612-1312
Tel: 559-323-2100, Fax: 559-323-5566
E-mail: jmorodomi@sjcl.edu
Web: www.sjcl.edu
Degrees Offered:
    Juris Doctor

Santa Barbara College of Law
20 E. Victoria Street
Santa Barbara, CA 93101
Tel: 805-966-0010, Fax: 805-966-7181
E-mail: sbcl@santabarbaralaw.edu
Web: www.santabarbaralaw.edu
Degrees Offered:
    Juris Doctor

Southern Calif. Institute of Law, Santa Barbara
1525 State Street, #202
Santa Barbara, CA 93101
Tel: 805-963-4654, Fax: 805-963-2367
E-mail: info@lawdegree.com
Web: www.lawdegree.com
Degrees Offered:
    Juris Doctor

Southern California Institute of Law, Ventura
877 South Victoria Ave., #111
Ventura, CA 93003
Tel: 805-644-2327, Fax: 805-963-2367
E-mail: info@lawdegree.com
Web: www.lawdegree.com
Degrees Offered:
　　Juris Doctor

Trinity Law School
2200 North Grand Avenue
Santa Ana, CA 92705
Tel: 714-836-7500, Fax: 714-796-7190
E-mail: tcdadm@tiu.edu
Web: www.tls.edu
Degrees Offered:
　　Juris Doctor

Ventura College of Law
4475 Market Street
Ventura, CA 93001
Tel: 805-658-0511, Fax: 805-658-0529
E-mail: vcl@venturalaw.edu
Web: www.venturalaw.edu
Degrees Offered:
　　Juris Doctor

University of West Los Angeles School of Law
1155 West Arbor Vitae Street
Inglewood, CA 90301-2902
Tel: 310-342-5200, Fax: Not Available
E-mail: info@uwla.edu
Web: www.uwla.edu
Degrees Offered:
　　Juris Doctor

University of La Verne College of Law
320 East "D" Street
Ontario, CA 91764-4128
Tel: 909-460-2000, Fax: 909-460-2081
E-mail: admissions@ulv.edu
Web: www.ulv.edu
Degrees Offered:
　　Juris Doctor

Massachusetts

Massachusetts School of Law
500 Federal Street
Andover, MA 01810
Tel: 978-681-0800, Fax: 978-681-6330
E-mail: mslaw@mslaw.edu
Web: www.mslaw.edu
Degrees Offered:
 Juris Doctor

Southern New England School of Law
333 Faunce Corner Road
North Dartmouth, MA 02747-1252
Tel: 800-213-0060, Fax: 508-998-9561
E-mail: acarreiro@snesl.edu
Web: www.snesl.edu
Degrees Offered:
 Juris Doctor

Tennessee

Nashville School of Law
2934 Sidco Drive
Nashville, TN 37204
Tel: 615-256-3684, Fax: 615-244-2383
E-mail: nashvilleschooloflaw@prodigy.net
Web: www.nashvilleschooloflaw.net
Degrees Offered:
 Juris Doctor

Unaccredited California Law Schools

Note: The same rules concerning admission to California distance-learning law schools and admission to the Bar are applicable to unaccredited California law schools. Therefore if you choose to attend one of the schools listed below you must comply with the rules of the State Bar of California as discussed in the previous chapter.

American College of Law
1717 South State College Blvd.
Suite 100
Anaheim, CA 92806
Tel: 714-634-3699, Fax: 714-634-3894
E-mail: info@aclaw.edu
Web: http://www.aclaw.com/
Degrees Offered:
 Juris Doctor

California Southern Law School
3775 Elizabeth Street
Riverside, CA 92506-2508
Tel: 909-683-6760, Fax: Not Available
E-mail: info@cslawschool.com
Web: http://www.cslawshcool.com/
Degrees Offered:
 Juris Doctor

Central California College of Law
1759 Fulton, Suite E4
Fresno, CA 93721
Tel: 559-233-4074, Fax: Not Available
E-mail: Not Available
Web: Not Available
Degrees Offered:
 Juris Doctor

Irvine University College of Law
10900 183rd Street, Suite 330
Cerritos, CA 90703
Tel: 562-865-7111, Fax: Not Available
E-mail: Not Available
Web: Not Available
Degrees Offered:
 Juris Doctor

Larry H. Layton School of Law
3807 West Sierra Highway, Suite 206
Acton, CA 93510
Tel: 661-269-5291, Fax: 661-269-5292
E-mail: laytonlaw@qnet.com
Web: http://www.vanguardnews.com/layton.htm
Degrees Offered:
 Juris Doctor

Note: If you live in the Acton CA area, Larry Layton runs an absolute superb program.

Oakland College of Law
120 Eleventh Street, Suite 103
Oakland, CA 94607-4806
Tel:510-832-5297, Fax: 510-832-5398
E-mail: Not Available
Web: Not Available
Degrees Offered:
     Juris Doctor

Pacific Coast University
College of Law
1650 Ximeno Avenue, Suite 310
Long Beach, CA 90804
Tel: 562-961-8200, Fax: 562-961-8215
E-mail: registrar@pculaw.com
Web: www.pculaw.com
Degrees Offered:
     Juris Doctor

Pacific West College of Law
2011 West Chapman Avenue
Orange, CA 92868
Tel: 714-634-3738, Fax: 714-634-2283
E-mail: admissions@pacificwestcollege.com
Web: www.pacificwestcollege.com
Degrees Offered:
     Juris Doctor

Peninsula University
College of Law
436 Dell Avenue
Mountain View, CA 94043
Tel: 650-964-5044, Fax: Not Available
E-mail: Not Available
Web: Not Available
Degrees Offered:
     Juris Doctor

People's College of Law
P.O. Box 57400
660 South Bonnie Brae Street
Los Angeles, CA 90057
Tel: 213-483-0083, Fax: 213-483-0593
E-mail: people@peoplescollegeoflaw.edu
Web: http://www.peoplescollegeoflaw.edu
Degrees Offered:
    Juris Doctor

Ridgecrest School of Law
115 North Balsam Street
Ridgecrest, CA 93555
Tel: 760-375-9005, Fax: Not Available
E-mail: Not Available
Web: Not Available
Degrees Offered:
    Juris Doctor

University of Northern California
Lorenzo Patino School of Law
1012 J Street
Sacramento, CA 95814
Tel: 916-447-7223, Fax: Not Available
E-mail: registrar@patinolawschool.com
Web: www.patinolawschool.com

Degrees Offered:
    Juris Doctor

Western Sierra Law School
8376 Hercules Street
La Mesa, CA 91942
Tel: 619-469-2245, Fax: Not Available
E-mail: Not Available
Web: Not Available
Degrees Offered:
    Juris Doctor

If you don't know where you're going,
when you get there you'll be lost.

Yogi Berra

Chapter VII

Lawyer Apprenticeship Programs

While it is not generally known or promoted, some U.S. states still permit one to be admitted to the bar after undergoing a number of years as a lawyer apprentice. At one time apprenticeship was the primary way, if not the only way, in which one could become a lawyer. Abraham Lincoln, Andrew Jackson, and Howard Taft, to name a few, are among the many U.S. presidents who became lawyers this way. In fact, until the middle of the 1900s, the majority of lawyers entered the profession by this route.

It seems obvious that the benefits of working side by side with experienced lawyers and judges should be welcomed by the traditional legal academic community. Sadly, however, this concept seems to be dying out rather than being capitalized upon. I believe the reason that traditional legal educators object to apprenticeship is the belief that it may not offer the apprentice a real opportunity to study the law in a broad manner and under controlled conditions. This argument has some merit, but it could, of course, also be argued that traditional law school does not adequately prepare students with the practical skills to enter the profession. Many new lawyers can tell you that they learned their craft after law school—and sometimes from their paralegal assistant.

One solution may be to compromise. Dr. Roger Agajanian, the founder of the Law School Apprentice Program, helps students find apprenticeships while cross-registering in good correspondence law schools. This way the apprentice/student gets both experiential and academic training. Dr. Agajanian, by the way, is the Dean of British American University, a high quality online and correspondence law school (See Chapter V).

> *"Apprenticeship also offers some unique features that are just not available with traditional education."*

Although no longer in vogue, apprenticeship still provides a viable route to becoming a practicing lawyer in some states. The rules vary quite a bit from state to state, for instance, New York requires that you first complete one year of study at an ABA- approved law school prior to becoming a lawyer apprentice while Vermont, California, and Virginia permit one to enter practice after four years of apprenticeship and passing the general bar examination. You'll want to review the specific requirements for each state's program to see if it's right for you, but in general, apprenticeships can be a great alternative to traditional legal education.

Apprenticeship also offers some unique features that are just not available with traditional education. Think about it, as an apprentice you have the opportunity to get valuable "hands on" experience working side by side with active and experienced practitioners. Let's take a quick look at the advantages of lawyer apprenticeship:

Advantages of Apprenticeship:

- You'll get valuable practical experience
- You'll get immediate responses to your questions from your mentor
- You'll get a well-balanced education
- You can concentrate right away in the specific area of practice that interests you
- You'll make valuable connections in the profession
- Generally flexible scheduling
- You'll save thousands of dollars over the cost of a traditional legal education
- You get paid to learn (sometimes)

There are currently nine states that permit lawyer apprentices to be admitted to the practice of law, they are as follows:

Alaska

Part I of the Rules for Admissions at Rule 2 Section 3(b) states: "An individual shall also be eligible to take the bar examination as a general applicant if he/she (1) has successfully completed not less than one academic year of education at a law school accredited or approved by the Council of Legal Education of the American Bar Association or the Association of American Law Schools, (2) has successfully completed a clerkship program. . . ."

Essentially this means that you must have successfully completed one year of full-time study at an ABA-approved law school before you can enter into an apprenticeship program.

California

Rule VII, Section 4 of the Rules Regulating Admission states: "The legal educational qualifications required of every general applicant . . . [include study] . . . in a law office in this state and under the personal supervision of a member of the State Bar of California, who is, and for at least five years continuously, has been engaged in the active practice of law . . . or . . . in the chambers and under the supervision of a judge of a court of record of this state. . . ."

What this means is that you can become a lawyer in California purely by completing four years as an apprentice and passing the general bar examination. Should you decide that this strategy is for you, I would highly recommend that you also enroll in an online or distance-learning law school to supplement your practical experience. For example, you may wish to enroll, for example, in the British American Law School, Concord Law School or, perhaps Saratoga Law School. (See Chapter V for a complete listing of U.S. online and correspondence law schools).

Maine

The Maine Bar Admission Rules at Rule 10(c)(5) states "[Each applicant must] . . . successfully complete two thirds of the requirements for graduation from a law school that had received its provisional or final accreditation from the American Bar Association by the time of the applicant's completion of those requirements and then within 12 months following such successful completion pursued the study of law in the law office of an attorney in the active practice of law in the state of Maine continuously on a full-time basis for at least one year; provided that the attorney must, in advance, present the proposed course of study to the board for its approval and, at its conclusion, certify that the course, as approved, was completed."

This will generally mean that you would need to have to first completed one year of full-time study of law at an ABA-approved law school prior to starting a lawyer apprenticeship program.

New York

The Rules for Admission of Attorneys and Counselors at Law, at Part 520.4(2) states " . . . that the applicant successfully completed at least one academic year as a matriculated student in a full-time program or the equivalent in a part-time program at an approved law school and at the conclusion thereof was eligible to continue in that school's degree program; and that the applicant thereafter studied law in a law office or offices located within New York State under the supervision of one or more attorneys admitted to practice law in New York State, for such period of time as, together with the credit allowed pursuant to this section for attendance in an approved law school, shall aggregate four years."

As with Alaska and Maine, New York requires that you successfully complete on year of legal academic study at an ABA approved law school before commencing a lawyer apprenticeship program.

Vermont

The Rules of Admission to the Bar of the Vermont Supreme Court, at Section 6(g) states that an applicant shall have pursued the study of law with special reference to the general practice of law:

> (1)   for a period of not less than four years within this state under the supervision of an attorney in practice in the state who has been admitted to practice before this Court not less than three years prior to the commencement of that study, or
>
> (2)   in any jurisdiction of the United States or common law jurisdiction in a law school approved by this Court which maintains a three-year course leading to a law degree.

This means that one may become a practicing attorney in Vermont purely by apprenticeship and without ever setting foot in a law school.

West Virginia

Rule 3.0(2)(a) of the Rules for Admission to Practice Law states "the applicant is a graduate of a non-ABA accredited law school, which school is of such stature that its graduates are eligible to take the bar exam of the state, District of Columbia, commonwealth or territory of the United States in which the law school is located, and

(b) The applicant has completed three (3) years of law office and work in this state as a legal assistant or paralegal, under the supervision of an attorney or attorneys admitted to practice in West Virginia, and provides to the Board a certification by the highest court of the state, District of Columbia, commonwealth or territory of the United States in which the law school is located that its graduates are eligible to take the bar examination of that jurisdiction. . . ."

West Virginia is unique in that the rules provide an avenue for graduates of non-ABA approved law schools to become members of the West Virginia Bar if they successfully complete a three year lawyer apprenticeship program. The key to taking advantage of this provision is that you must be eligible to take the bar examination in your particular law school's jurisdiction.

Virginia

The Code of Virginia, 1950, as amended, at Section 54.1-3926, authorized a lawyer apprenticeship program known as the "Law Reader Program."

According to the Virginia Board of Bar Examiners, "[t]he law reader program is intended to provide an alternative legal education for people who, although otherwise qualified for admission to law school, are, by reason of various circumstances, unable to take or complete a law school course of study. The program is not intended for persons who are unable, by reason of academic, aptitude, or other deficiencies, to obtain admission to an approved law school. The program is designed to supply, in combination, a theoretical, scholastic and clinical experience."

If approved, successful candidates will undergo three years of intensive apprenticeship under the supervision of a Virginia attorney.

I particularly like Virginia's apprenticeship program because it recognizes that law study is not for everyone and therefore limits the program to candidates who would otherwise be qualified to attend an ABA-approved school. This avoids wasting the time (and perhaps money) of persons who really have no business studying law. The downside is that you must take the LSAT, an examination that some argue is not indicative of one's ability or probable success in law school. Still, the Virginia Board of Bar Examiners should be applauded for offering a wonderful alternative to traditional law school without sacrificing high standards.

Washington

Rule 6 of the State Bar of Washington Admission to practice states at subsection 3 "Every applicant shall . . . obtain regular full term employment in the State of Washington as a law clerk with (i) a judge of a court of general or appellate jurisdiction, or (ii) a lawyer or a firm of lawyers licensed to practice in this state and actively engaged in the practice of law; (4) submit on forms provided by the Bar Association (i) an application for admission to the law clerk program, (ii) the tutor's statement . . . (5) appear for an interview . . . (c) Length of Study . . . Four calendar years: Each calendar year shall consist of at least 48 weeks with a minimum of 30 hours study each week"

In addition the apprentice must take monthly written examinations, administered and graded by the tutor. And the apprentice must appear before the Board of Governors at least once per year for an evaluation of their academic progress.

Washington offers a great "full" apprenticeship program with good built-in controls to protect the apprentice from pursuing a career he or she is not suited for, and, to assure that only qualified apprentices are permitted to take the general bar examination.

Wyoming

Rule 202 of the Rules and Procedures Governing Admission to Practice of Law provides for up to two years credit for an approved lawyer apprenticeship program. Section (a)(2) states that "[t]he time of study in the office of a member of the Wyoming State Bar or judge, showing the actual period of such study, together with a listing and description of the substantive topics of law studied. Evidence of tests taken, as well as written material, may be requested. . . ."

This means in effect that you must complete at least one year of full-time study at an ABA-approved law school before commencing an apprenticeship program.

Summary

There are currently nine states that have viable apprenticeship programs that are worth considering. However, you must consider that with Alaska, Maine, New York, and Wyoming you must generally first complete one year of full-time study at an ABA-approved law school. Remember, that to be admitted to an ABA-approved school, you must have a strong undergraduate GPA, take and score well on the LSAT exam and make the cut of the admission's committee. Most students who are accepted to and make it through their first year of law school are well advised to stay the course and work hard to graduate. However, sometimes, things don't always work out the way you planned and you might find that, due to financial hardships or personal issues, you have to drop out. For such individuals, these states offer a wonderful opportunity.

Five states offer full apprenticeship programs, as follows: California,

Vermont, Virginia, Washington, and West Virginia. If you live in or near one of these states you may want to consider an apprenticeship program. In these states you can actually do your entire legal study under the supervision of a judge or lawyer. As wonderful an opportunity as this may be, I would still highly recommend that you enroll in a distance learning or online law school to supplement your program. The reason? Bar examinations are quite difficult and you will need a great academic foundation—take every edge you can get!

A Final Word of Caution

The specific rules for lawyer apprenticeship programs vary somewhat from state to state and, like all rules, are subject to change without notice. If you are considering an apprenticeship program, be certain to contact the Bar Association of the particular state you are interested in to get a copy of the most current requirements. A complete list of state Bar Associations and contact information may be found in Appendix A.

Education is what survives when what has been learned has been forgotten.

B. F. Skinner

Chapter VIII

Crossing the Border: Getting Admitted in the State of Your Choice

Options For Nontraditional Law Graduates

If you have persevered and earned your law degree by an alternative method of study, it's a good indication that you have what it takes to be a lawyer. You will have worked hard and learned that alternative legal education does not mean watered down and that you can therefore proudly stand side-by-side with your colleagues. But now comes the time to prepare to sit for the bar examination. Because you earned your degree by non-traditional means, that is, by attending a foreign law school or U.S. unaccredited law school or by distance learning, you will not be able to take the bar exam in every state, however, you still have many options.

Options for Foreign Law School Graduates

Many U.S. states will permit foreign law graduates to sit for their bar exam after meeting certain prerequisites. This can vary from state to state, with some states granting full recognition to foreign law degrees (often after a petition and evaluation), to requiring the candidate to earn an LL.M degree from an ABA-approved law school. Even where you choose to apply to a state that requires you to obtain an LL.M, before sitting for their bar examination, you will find that this is not as overwhelming as it might first seem. First of all, many ABA law schools now offer LL.M programs and a few of them may be earned completely online. Moreover, there is generally very little competition to get admitted to LL.M programs and there are no

LSATs, standardized tests or other barriers to admission as there are with the J.D. degree. Finally, if you obtain this prestigious degree you will be among an elite 3% of American lawyers who hold such an advanced law degree and, depending on the school you choose, your overall tuition costs will generally be much lower than the cost of a full J.D. degree.

The key to the whole process is to get admitted in one state, any state, even if it's not the actual state you ultimately wish to practice in. Why? Because once you're admitted in one state other states may permit you to be admitted by reciprocity, petition or by virtue of your being admitted in another state for a period of time, typically three to five years. Oddly enough, many lawyers are admitted in one state while working as a lawyer for a law firm in a completely different state. This often takes place in interstate law firms with the "local" attorney acting in a supervisory role. You'll want to check on any particular restrictions in your desired jurisdiction, but this multi-jurisdictional practice is actually quite common.

The following states offer the most reasonable admissions and reciprocity policies for foreign law graduates:

Alaska

Alaska will permit many foreign law school graduates from common law countries to sit for its bar examination if they complete one academic year at an ABA-approved law school including courses in U.S. Constitution Law and Federal Civil Procedure.

Alabama

Foreign law school graduates may petition the Alabama Supreme Court to take the bar examination.

California

The State Bar of California will require you to have an evaluation of your foreign law school transcript(s) before considering your application to sit for the general bar exam (See Chapter II). Generally this will result in your being credited with some applicable credit that may permit you to bypass the baby bar exam. It is more likely, however, that you will have to take some additional credits and possibly pass the baby bar exam prior to taking the general bar exam. This is not as bad as it might seem. The additional credits you need can be acquired by distance learning from a State Bar registered online or correspondence law school and taking the baby bar can actually be good practice for the "real thing"—think of it as a form of bar review.

Connecticut

Connecticut may permit foreign law graduates to sit for their bar exam upon earning an LL.M degree at an ABA law school. The good news is that many ABA law schools offer LL.M programs and there is very little competition for placement in these programs (and no LSAT or similar entrance examinations.) (See Appendix C for a list of ABA-approved law schools offering LL.M programs.) Also, Connecticut requires that the foreign law degree be obtained from a law school in a common law country. (Such as the foreign law schools listed in this book).

District of Columbia

Applicants with foreign law degrees may sit for the D.C. bar exam upon successful completion of 26 semester hours at an ABA law school. This can be an LL.M, but the subjects studied must be those subjects tested on the D.C. bar exam.

Louisiana

Foreign law school graduates may have their law school transcript(s) evaluated and, if found to be equivalent, will be issued a certificate of equivalency authorizing them to sit for the bar exam.

Massachusetts

Massachusetts may permit foreign law school graduates depending on the particular content of the legal study undertaken.

Michigan

Michigan will permit foreign law graduates to sit for the bar exam if they obtain an LL.M. from an ABA law school. (See Appendix C)

New Hampshire

New Hampshire will permit foreign law graduates to sit for the bar exam if they obtain an LL.M. from an ABA law school. (See Appendix C)

New York

New York will permit many foreign law school graduates from common law countries to sit for its bar examination. Candidates who do not qualify or whose law degree was earned in a non-common law country may sit for the bar exam after obtaining 20 semester credits from an ABA-approved law school. Note, however, that if your degree was earned by distance leaning, New York may still deny you based on the curious wording under Rule 520. Notwithstanding, you can petition the New York State Court of Appeals to take the exam. (See Appendix C)

North Carolina

North Carolina will permit foreign law graduates to sit for the bar exam if they obtain an LL.M. from an ABA law approved school by August 2005. (See Appendix C)

Ohio

Ohio will permit foreign law school graduates to sit for the bar examination after their law school transcript(s) are evaluated and determined by the Ohio Supreme Court to be substantially equivalent to an ABA-approved law school education. In the event that it is not, you will generally be required to take some additional subjects at an ABA-approved law school.

Puerto Rico

Puerto Rico may permit a foreign law graduate to sit for its bar exam if the applicant petitions the court and takes four additional subjects at an ABA-approved law school.

Rhode Island

Rhode Island will permit foreign law graduates to sit for the bar exam if they obtain an LL.M. from an ABA law school. (See Appendix C)

Tennessee

Foreign law school graduates may take the Tennessee bar exam if their foreign law study is determined to be substantially equivalent to legal study at an ABA-approved law school.

Texas

Foreign law school graduates may take the Texas bar exam if they obtain an LL.M degree from an ABA law school. However, this applies only if the foreign degree was not earned by distance learning. (See Appendix C)

Virginia

Virginia will permit foreign law graduates to sit for the bar exam if they obtain an LL.M. from an ABA law school. (See Appendix C)

Washington

Washington will permit a foreign law graduate to sit for the bar exam if they participate in a three-year apprenticeship program.

For a current detailed list of rules check with the particular state in which you are seeking to be admitted. (See Appendix A)

Options for Graduates of Unaccredited U.S. Law Schools

If you obtained your law degree from a non-ABA approved law school in the United States, such as from a law school in Alabama, Massachusetts, Tennessee, or even from a California distance-learning law school, you can be admitted in that particular state if you successfully pass the bar examination and meet the administrative and moral character prerequisites. If you want to practice in a different state you have several options:

- Apply for admission on motion to states that have liberal reciprocity agreements.
- Apply for admission by examination to states that permit attorneys licensed in other states to sit for their bar examination.
- Practice for a period of time (normally 3 to 5 years) and then apply to be admitted by motion to another state.
- Practice for a period of time (normally 3 to 5 years) and then apply to be admitted by examination to another state.

Once you are admitted in one state, other states will permit you be admitted in their states by reciprocity agreement, by petition or by fulfilling a waiting period, commonly three to five years. As indicated above, many lawyers are admitted in one state while working as a lawyer for a law firm in a completely different state. Most states will even permit lawyers licensed in one state to be partners in a law firm in their states. Again, you'll want to check on any particular restrictions in your jurisdiction as the regulations can change and vary from state to state. (See Appendix A for a list of State Bar Associations)

Reciprocity

Some states have very liberal reciprocity policies and will admit any lawyer if they are licensed in any other U.S. state or territory (e.g., Vermont, Washington, West Virginia, and the District of Columbia). Many other states also have liberal reciprocity agreements but require that the state you are licensed in also permit its lawyers full reciprocity. Depending on the state you would ultimately wish to practice law in, you may wish to be admitted in a jurisdiction that has an "open" reciprocity policy. Utilizing this strategy you would first be admitted in a state that permits graduates of non-ABA approved law schools to sit for the bar examination and then apply for admission in a jurisdiction such as the District of Columbia, which has a large number of reciprocity agreements. Once this is achieved you will have many more options to be admitted in other states. Again, you will need to check with the state bar authorities to determine the current reciprocity agreements and for any particular rules that may apply (See Appendix A)

Practice Requirements

Some states, in addition to or in place of full reciprocity policies will require that you be licensed and in the practice of law for a period of time before applying for admission. The usual practice period is three to five years depending on the particular state, but can be longer.

Listed below are states that require a specific waiting period for graduates of non-ABA approved law schools:

Alaska

Five years of active practice in another jurisdiction.

Arizona

Five years of active practice in another jurisdiction.

California

If you are admitted in another state you should be permitted to sit for the bar in California.

Colorado

Five years of active practice in another jurisdiction and your law degree must be from a state approved/accredited law school.

Florida

Ten years of active practice in another jurisdiction.

Hawaii

Five years of active practice in another jurisdiction.

Kentucky

No specific practice period but you must submit your law school transcripts/records for an evaluation.

Maine

Three years of active practice in another jurisdiction.

Missouri

Five years of active practice in another jurisdiction.

New York

Five years of active practice in another jurisdiction.

New Mexico

Four years of active practice in another jurisdiction.

Oregon

Three years of active practice in another jurisdiction.

Pennsylvania

Five years of active practice in another jurisdiction.

Texas

Three years of active practice in another jurisdiction. However, Texas will not permit graduates of correspondence law schools.

Again, for a current detailed list of rules check with the particular state in which you are seeking to be admitted. (See Appendix A)

Other Strategies

There are many lawyers who are licensed in one jurisdiction and are working as attorneys for law firms in states that they are not actually licensed in. This is true irrespective of whether they graduated from an ABA approved law school or an unaccredited school. Lawyers from different states sometimes form law firms with partners licensed in different states. Attorneys in these situations are working in their profession every day and even represent clients, make appearances and do pretty much everything any other lawyer does on a daily basis. Some states have a limitation on the number of years they will permit you to work (practice) in their state before requiring you to get a license there.

Federal Practice

Additionally, some lawyers limit their practice to certain areas of federal law such as Immigration Law, Taxation, Social Security, Patent and Trademark Law, etc. State Bar Associations should take the position that federal supremacy provides for U.S. government regulation of practice in these areas and that lawyers from other states should be permitted to practice in these areas notwithstanding that they are not members of the Bar in the particular state they are actually practicing. Still, you should check with the appropriate State authorities to be sure you comply with the laws and rules governing such practice. (See Appendix A)

Earning A LL.M Degree

Some students prefer to earn an LL.M degree after obtaining their J.D. from an unaccredited law school. The LL.M is a Master of Laws degree and is offered in many legal specializations or in a general legal discipline. The reasons for obtaining a LL.M degree vary from person to person, however, some feel that their degree is tainted by the fact that it is "unaccredited," notwithstanding the actual high quality of their course of legal education—it's a matter of perception. Whatever the reasoning, there can be a great deal of value in earning a LL.M after a J.D. degree. For one thing only 3 % of all U.S. lawyers have an LL.M degree. This can be particularly useful in broadening your employment options, particularly if you choose a specialization such as tax law, medical malpractice, intellectual property or many other areas where specialized legal knowledge is important.

> *"For one thing only 3 % of all U.S. lawyers have an LL.M degree. This can be particularly useful in broadening your employment options..."*

Another advantage is that you can actually accelerate your legal education. For example, if you choose to enroll in a California correspondence law school and wish to comply with Rule 20 you will follow a course of study for four years, which would include taking the difficult baby bar exam after your first year of study. However, although California offers the most liberal legal study options, it also has the most difficult bar examination in the country and, not everyone wants to practice law in California anyway. As such, some students elect to accelerate their studies and complete their J.D. by distance learning in three and in some cases two years and then enroll in an ABA-approved LL.M program for one or two years. This provides them with three distinct advantages:

1) They earn a joint degree (JD/LL.M) in three to four years

2) They save thousands of dollars over the cost of a traditional law degree

3) They can take the bar exam in several states other than California

Of course, if a student does not initially comply with California's Rule 20, it means that they cannot sit for the California bar exam after earning their J.D. degree, however, they may later apply to sit for the general bar exam after obtaining their LL.M degree.

In addition, many states do not have a published policy of permitting holders of ABA-approved LL.M degrees to sit for their exam, however, in practice, they will often permit such applicants to sit for their bar exam after filing a petition. My advice is to apply, and if you're turned down, file a petition to be admitted or to be permitted to sit for the general bar examination.

Obtaining an LL.M cannot only increase your marketability and employability in the profession, but it often constitutes an integral part of your strategy to being admitted to the bar. To assist you in selecting the appropriate LL.M program, should you decide this is necessary or desirable, I have listed ABA-approved law schools offering such programs in Appendix C.

Can you practice law without being admitted to the bar?

The answer to this question is a resounding NO! Don't even think about it, it would be illegal and would likely hamper your future goals of becoming a licensed attorney. In short, don't do it. That being said, it is not always clear what exactly is meant by the "practice of law." For example, if you went up to a school crossing guard and asked him if it was legal to cross the street in the middle of the block and he responded "no" (or yes), isn't he giving legal advice? Now I agree that this is an extreme example, but I do want to make a point that there is a wide range of room to differ about where the practice of law begins and ends. Be aware of this and please refrain from coming near the dividing line between activities that are reserved solely for licensed attorneys and those activities permissible for paraprofessionals.

There are some very lawyer-like activities that are permitted for laypersons and paraprofessionals and you are free to engage in these activities without fear of violating the law. The vast majority of these career options are made available under federal law and some can provide you with a very good standard of living and/or serve as a practical training ground for you while you are pursuing you legal studies. For those of you who are interested in a quasi-legal career, you can "practice" in one of the following special areas, provided that you fully comply with rules and you do not misrepresent your position.

> *"There are some very lawyer-like activities that are permitted for laypersons and paraprofessionals and you are free to engage in these activities without fear of violating the law."*

Practice Before the United States Tax Court

Title XX of the Tax Court Rules provides for non-attorneys to practice before the U.S. Tax Courts. Many non-attorney practitioners earn a very good living representing others in the complex area of tax law. But, not everyone can do this. You must take a very difficult examination known unofficially as the "Tax Bar Examination."

And don't take the exam lightly, it is quite difficult indeed and, you must know not only tax law, but also, contract law, federal rules of civil procedure, and the federal rules of evidence. If you successfully pass the examination and meet the administrative and moral character standards, you can carve out a very rewarding and profitable career as a practitioner—albeit not an attorney. For more information contact the U.S. Tax Court:

U.S. Tax Court
400 Second Street, N.W.
Washington, D.C. 20217
Tel: 202-606-8736
Web: http://www.ustaxcourt.gov/ustcweb.htm&e=747

Irrespective of how well you know the subjects tested on the tax bar examination, I urge you to seek the help of good prep course. For the Tax Bar there is only one that I can recommend, MaxsTaxes. Contact Mary Ann at the number below, she is a wealth of information and unrivaled in her field.

Max's Taxes
1450 Kingswood Drive, Suite 348
Roseville, CA 95678-7903
Tel: 916-772-7444, Fax: 916-772-7445
E-mail: max@maxstaxes.com
Web: http://www.maxstaxes.com/

Practice before the United States Patent and Trademark Office

The Rules of Practice for patent and trademark cases is set forth in 37 CFR sections 10.5, 10.6 and 10.7. These rules provide for non-attorney practitioners, called agents, who are permitted to do nearly everything an attorney can with the exception of representing a person before the USPTO tribunal. In the PTO world that means you can do about 95% of everything a PTO attorney can do. Follow the rules and learn your craft well and you can have an extremely lucrative practice. However, just as with the Tax Court, you must know this area well and have a strong academic background in the sciences and mathematics—and you have to pass an exam.

For more information about becoming an agent/practitioner contact the USPTO:

U.S. Patent and Trademark Office
Crystal Plaza 3, Room 2C02
Washington, DC 20231
Tel: 800-786-9199 or 703-308-4357
E-mail: usptoinfo@uspto.gov
Web: http://www.uspto.gov/web/offices/dcom/olia/oed/

Immigration and Naturalization Service

The Immigration and Naturalization Service, an agency of the U.S. Department of Justice, also provides for non-attorney practitioners under 8 CFR section 103.2. Under the INS rules, a non-attorney practitioner is known as a "representative" and may even represent persons before INS hearings and certain tribunals. Typically, the representative will work for some private organization, for example, immigrant rights organizations. The process of obtaining authorization to appear on behalf of clients is quite simple compared to the stringent rules of the U.S. Tax court and USPTO, but you will want to gain competence in immigration law and law in general before representing clients in matters that are extremely important to them. And yes, you can be sued for malpractice. If you would like more information about being a representative contact the INS:

Immigration and Naturalization Service
USINS Washington District Office
4420 N. Fairfax Drive
Arlington, VA 22203
Web: http://www.ins.usdoj.gov/graphics/index.htm

Social Security Administration

Social Security Disability Advocates: 42 U.S.C. 404.1705(b) provides for non-attorney representation of Social Security disability claimants. So long as you comply with the rules set forth for such representation and do not represent yourself as an attorney you may lawfully establish a Social Security "practice."

Social Security Administration
6401 Security Blvd.,
Baltimore, MD 21235-0001
Tel: 800-772-1213
Web: http://www.ssa.gov/oha/inforep.htm

Federal Trade Commission
600 Pennsylvania Avenue
N.W., Washington, D.C. 20580
Tel: 202-326-2222
Web: http://www.ftc.gov/

Far travel, very far travel, or travail, comes near to the worth of staying at home.

Henry David Thoreau

Chapter IX

Practicing Law In Other Countries

Canada

The legal profession in Canada is governed by one of the fourteen law societies of Canada. In general, the education requirements to practice law in Canada may be satisfied by one of the two following methods:

a) Obtain a LL.B degree from an accredited Canadian law school
b) Obtain a LL.B from a fully accredited non-Canadian law school

Graduates of the accredited law programs listed in this book who have earned a LL.B degree (or J.D.) would be eligible if they obtained their degree under method "b" and would be required to submit transcripts of their legal education and experience, if any, to the National Committee on Accreditation (NCA) for evaluation. Each case is reviewed individually, but typically candidates can expect to be required take some or all of the following additional courses:

- Administrative
- Constitution Law
- Corporate Law
- Evidence
- Tax Law

According to the Federation of Law Societies of Canada, the following factors are considered in determining the additional education required to meet the legal education requirements for the practice of law in Canada:

- Age of the degree
- Academic Standing of the Student
- The particular subjects studied
- The undergraduate education of the candidate

According to the NCA, "candidates with Upper Second Class Honours should receive "advanced standing as would a candidate with Lower Second Class Honours, though not as much. Third Class standing or lower normally will not receive any advanced standing."

Therefore, you may be required to obtain ten additional credits, which is roughly equivalent to 1.5 years of additional study. Not bad if you consider that the LL.B degree may be earned in two or three years by distance learning—and at a fraction of the cost of traditional U.S. and Canadian Law Schools.

Once the NCA makes a determination on the additional courses a candidate must undertake, the candidate then has a choice of two methods to fulfill the requirements:

1) Study at an accredited Canadian Law School
2) Take a private course under the auspices of the NCA

Many U.S. and Canadian students are working full time and simply cannot afford to quit their jobs to attend a full-time program. And, part-time law schools are not generally available in Canada. However, by utilizing the alternative legal education strategies in this book Canadian and U.S. law students (and students from any country) can become a Canadian lawyer—and save not only time, but also thousands of dollars over the traditional method of becoming a lawyer. And, recall, outside the U.S., distance learning law programs are quite the norm.

United Kingdom

The legal profession in the United Kingdom is a bifurcated system made up of Solicitors and Barristers. In the past, only barristers were afforded audience privileges, that is, they were able to appear before the court. Solicitors, on the other hand, prepared cases for trial and tended to other legal matters handled outside the courtroom. Today, many solicitors also have rights of audience and there is much discussion about merging the two classes.

Qualification as a Solicitor:

- Step 1 Obtain a Qualifying Law Degree
- Step 2 Complete a Legal Practice Course (LPC)
- Step 3 Training Contract

Candidates who have earned an LL.B degree from one of the accredited law schools listed in this book will generally meet the requirements of Step 1. Your degree will be on equal footing irrespective of whether it was earned by classroom study or by distance learning. It must, however, be conferred by an accredited law school. Step 2 may be completed by enrolling in a one-year full time course, two-year part time course or by distance learning. Step 3 is fulfilled by undergoing an apprenticeship period with a Solicitor firm.

U.S. Lawyers Wishing to Qualify as U.K. and Commonwealth Solicitors

Any U.S. licensed attorney may become accredited to practice law in the United Kingdom by passing the Qualified Lawyers Transfer Test (QLTT), administered by the Law Society. Examinations are administered in New York, Chicago and Los Angeles. A U.S. attorney must be licensed to practice in one of the 50 United States, and have at least two years legal practice experience.

Attorneys with less than two years practice may still take the QLTT examination but need to apply for deferred licensing following proof of two years practice experience.

For more information visit: **www.qltt.com/index.htm**

Qualification as a Barrister:

- Step 1 Obtain a Qualifying Law Degree
- Step 2 Gain Admission to an Inns of Court
- Step 3 Complete a Bar Vocational Course (BVC)
- Step 4 Complete a Six Month Pupillage
- Step 5 Obtain a Provisional Practising Certificate
- Step 6 Complete a Six Month Pupillage
- Step 7 Obtain a Practising Certificate as a Barrister

As with the Requirements for Solicitors, candidates who have obtained a LL.B degree from one of the accredited law schools listed in this book the will generally meet the requirements of Step 1. Step 2 may be completed by attending the prescribed number of dinners at an Inns of Court. Step 3 may be completed by completing a one-year full-time or two year part-time BVC course. Steps 4 to 7 are completed by obtaining a pupillage (apprenticeship) with a chamber of Barristers for two six-month intervals and upon meeting with satisfactory approval, being issued a Practising Certificate.

Caribbean

Procedure for Admittance to Practice Law

In 1970, fourteen Caribbean nations, along with the Cayman Islands, formed the Council of Legal Education. The Council's primary function was to promulgate rules of practice and to establish the minimum standards of legal education for lawyers wishing to practice law before the courts of the member states. The following Caribbean nations are signatories to the agreement.

Antigua	Guyana
Bahamas	Jamaica
Barbados	Montserrat
British Honduras	St. Kitts-Nevis-Anguilla
British Virgin Islands	St. Lucia
Cayman Islands	St. Vincent

Dominica   Trinidad and Tobago
Grenada

There are two methods of meeting the Council's requirements:

1) Obtain a LL.B degree from the University of the West
   Indies
2) Obtain a LL.B degree from a fully accredited institution

Candidates who have obtained a LL.B degree from one of the accredited law schools listed in this book the will generally meet the requirements of Step 1 and would then need to apply for admission to a short program at one of the following three law schools established by the Council:

Norman Manley Law School
Jamaica

Hugh Wooding Law School
Trinidad

Eugene Dupuch Law School
Bahamas

Once admitted to one of the Council's law schools, candidates will undertake a course of study in the laws of the Caribbean followed by a short apprenticeship with a Caribbean law firm. Upon meeting these requirements, the candidate will be awarded a "Legal Education Certificate" certifying that he or she has successfully fulfilled the education and training requirements for admission to practice. No person is permitted to practice in the Caribbean without being awarded this certificate.

Some nontraditional law-school graduates may wish to be admitted in the Caribbean first before seeking admission to practice in the U.S., UK or Canada as it is often easier to be admitted elsewhere once admitted in another common law jurisdiction. I should also remind you that earning a law degree by distance learning is actually quite common in the UK, Caribbean and, to some extent, Canada—

to this extent it is really not nontraditional at all. These programs are only nontraditional from a U.S. perspective, and even then, only for the past 50 years or so.

*[The shortage of student loans] may require ...
divestiture of certain sorts—stereo divestiture,
automobile divestiture, three-weeks-at-the-beach
divestiture.*

*—William J. Bennett
U.S. Secretary of Education*

Chapter X

Financing Your Legal Education

Scholarships

Depending on your budget and particular financial situation, you may want to consider the possibility of financing your legal education or, perhaps, if you are fortunate, getting a full or partial scholarship to pay for your education. Since most scholarships are offered as a grant or gift, they need never to be paid back. This, then, should be your first step when considering methods to pay for your education. Surprisingly, there are a wide variety of sources for education grants available from organizations, corporations, foundations, and individuals.

The first step in learning of the many grants and scholarships available is to visit your local public library. Go to the reference section and locate the *Grants Register*. This book will list almost every grant and scholarship available, the application requirements, and contact information of the award-granting body. Some of the scholarships have some unusual and sometimes bizarre requirements, but many are fairly straightforward. Spend some time going through the book, if you obtain a scholarship it will have been well worth it. To give you a glimpse of the scope of scholarships available, take a look at the following examples:

- **National Civilian Community Corps**
  1100 Vermont Avenue NW
  Washington, DC 20525
  Tel: 800-942-2677
  Web: http://americorps.org
  NCCC offers tuition scholarships in exchange for 11 months of service.

- **American Association of University Women**
  2201 N Dodge Street
  Iowa City, IA 52243-4030
  Tel: 319-337-1716
  AAUW offers a wide variety of scholarships and grants for women.

- **HEATH**
  One Dupont Circle, Suite 800
  Washington, DC 20036-1193
  Tel: 800-544-3284
  HEATH offers scholarships for students with disabilities.

- **American Indian College Fund**
  8333 Greenwood Blvd.
  Denver, CO 80221
  303-426-1200
  Scholarships for Native Americans

- **Veterans Administration**
  Tel: 877-823-2378
  Grants for veterans under the GI Bill

- **Gates Millennium Scholars Fund**
  P.O. Box 10500
  Fairfax, VA 22031-8044
  Web: www.gmsp.org
  Tel: 877-690-6477
  Offers grants and scholarships for minority students

And this list is by no means exhaustive. One of the more unusual grants that I came across is for students being "the second child of Irish immigrants." The list is endless!

Don't overlook your employer as a source of scholarship money. Many firms and companies large and small have scholarship programs or will consider one on a case-by-case basis for their employees. Some may require that you maintain certain grades and/or that you agree to continue working for the company for a particular period of time, but such conditions are usually more than reasonable. Many companies will pay not only your tuition fees but will often cover the costs of books and transportation. You have absolutely nothing to lose by asking your employer to pay for your education, it is a win-win arrangement.

> **"Many companies will pay not only your tuition fees but will often cover the costs of books and transportation."**

Finding the money for law school or college is a major problem for students and parents today. Even though there are Billions of dollars worth of Scholarships available, finding them can be like finding the proverbial needle in a haystack, right? Well, an interesting resource, The Scholarship & Grant Guide eliminates this nightmare. **The Scholarship & Grant Guide is available at www.MariluxPress.com.**

Other sources of scholarships can be found on the Internet. Just go to any reliable search engine like www.google.com or a directory such as www.yahoo.com and enter the search term "scholarship," you will find hundreds if not thousands of sources. One notable source for finding scholarship money is www.finaid.com. Finaid has a search function that will match you with the many scholarships that you may qualify for. The way this works is that you fill out an online form with your particular academic, financial, and personal information. Based on your particulars, the program will search a database for the most suitable matches. This is a great service and can save you a lot of time over applying for scholarships and grants that you have no chance of getting. But if you have the time, you should really look through the *Grants Registry* first.

There are also a number or fee-based scholarship search services that claim to have a high success rate in matching students with scholarships. If you are desperate and do not have the time to look for scholarship money yourself you might want to try a fee-based service.

Loans for U.S. Non-ABA Law School Students

For U.S. unaccredited law schools you will probably not be eligible for federally guaranteed deferred student loans, such as the Stafford Loan. However, you can apply for private loans to fund your education, for example, from your local bank. Additionally, almost every U.S. law school listed in this book offers some form of direct or third party financing program allowing you to make monthly payments. And remember, that many of these schools offer a low annual tuition fee of ranging from $1,500.00 to $5,000.00 per year. A number of these schools have scholarship programs as well, which can further reduce your tuition burden.

What Is A Deferred Loan?

A deferred loan is a loan that you do not have to begin paying back until approximately nine months after you graduate. This is a godsend for many students because they can concentrate on their studies while they are pursuing their law degree and worry about paying for their education after they have commenced their professional career as a lawyer. In addition the interest rates are very competitive and you can extend the payment period for up to 25 years. If eligible, you may borrow up to $15,000.00 per year without a co-borrower—which should be more then ample for the majority of schools listed in Chapter III.

Even If you decide to attend a school that is not approved for guaranteed student loans, you will generally find that education in countries outside the United States is a bargain. You may be charged an additional fee as a foreign student, but you will probably be paying less than half the cost of a traditional U.S. ABA law school education. And don't forget you may still be eligible for a private loan and, perhaps, even a grant or scholarship.

To receive more information about guaranteed student loans or to obtain an application, please visit the U.S. Department of Education's website at www.fafsa.ed.gov/.

International Student Loan Programs

Many students thinking about enrolling in and attending a foreign law school are surprised to learn that in many cases they are eligible for the Stafford Loan, a federally guaranteed deferred student loan. To be eligible for the Stafford Loan, you must be a U.S. citizen or resident and be enrolled in a college or university that has been approved by the U.S. Department of Education. Surprisingly, the U.S. Department of Education not only approves U.S. schools, but also approves many foreign schools throughout the world. In fact, at the time of this writing there are well over 500 such schools. Many of these schools have law-degree programs. If you are interested in pursuing studies abroad at a foreign law school, please go back to Chapter III and check the list for foreign law schools you are interested in attending. I have listed the U.S. Federal Student Loan Code for each school that has been approved by the U.S. Education Department.

Lotteries

If I told you to try and win the lottery to help pay for your legal education you would probably think I was joking, or perhaps that I've taken leave of my senses, right? Well, that's exactly what I am saying and I'm not joking or crazy, here's why. All websites need visitors to their sites to survive. These visitors, or traffic as it is called in the trade, are the life-blood of dot-com businesses. Just like with traditional local businesses, if nobody visits the store, the owner will soon go broke. Merchants know that statistically, an increase in the amount of traffic to their business corresponds with an increase in sales—more traffic equals more sales.

Internet businesses operate in much the same way as traditional businesses and conduct their business according to the same principle, that is, more traffic equals more sales. Some bright website owner decided to offer Scholarship Lotteries in order to get people to visit the site and it worked and worked well. When an idea works so well, there's going to be others who want to duplicate their success and that is exactly what happened here, and you could be the winner. Sure the odds are that you won't win, but even with a 1 in 10,000 chance, why not try? It's completely free to play and as they say, "hey you never know."

Below are some of the more popular online scholarship lottery programs:

- www.iWon.com
- www.GoldPocket.com
- http://www.freescholarships.com/
- www.Jackpot.com
- www.VarsityBooks.com

Again, there are no guarantees that you will win so you will want to look to traditional sources of scholarship money and student loans such as those listed above. Also be sure to visit **www.MaxStudy.com** frequently to find the most current sources of student loans and scholarships.

Finally, there are some worthwhile books about obtaining scholarships available at **www.MariluxPress.com**.

The Scholarship Guide – Jerry Bohlken

The College Board Scholarship Handbook - The College Board

Winning Scholarships for College - Marianne Ragins

8 Steps to Help Black Families Pay For College - Thomas LaVeist

Appendix A

List of United States Bar Associations

UNITED STATES

American Bar Association (ABA)
750 N. Lake Shore Drive
Chicago, IL 60611
Tel: 312-988-5000
Web: www.abanet.org

Federal Bar Association
2215 M Street, N.W.
Washington, C.C. 20037
Tel: 202-785-1614, Fax (202) 785-1568
Web: fba@fedbar.org

State Bar Associations

Alabama State Bar

P.O. Box 671
415 Dexter Avenue, Montgomery, AL, 36104
Tel: 334-269-1515, Fax: 334-261-6310
Web: http://www.alabar.org/

Alaska Bar Association

P.O. Box 100279
510 L Street #602
Anchorage, AK 99510
Tel: 907-272-7469, Fax: 907-272-2932.
Web: http://www.alaskabar.org

Arizona - State Bar of Arizona
111 W. Monroe Street, Suite 1800
Phoenix, AZ 85003-1742
Tel: 602-340-7200, Fax: 602-271-4930
Web: http://www.azbar.org

Arkansas State Bar Association
400 W. Markham, Suite 401
Little Rock, AR 72201
Tel: 501-375-4605, Fax: 501-375-4901
Web: http://www.arkbar.com

California State Bar Association
555 Franklin Street
San Francisco, CA 94102
Tel: 415-561-8200, Fax: 415-561-8305
Web: http://www.calbar.org

Colorado Bar Association
1900 Grant Street, #950
Denver, CO 80203
Tel: 303-860-1115, Fax: 303-894-0821
Web: http://www.cobar.org

Connecticut State Bar Association
101 Corporate Place
Rocky Hill, CT 06067
Tel: 860-721-0025, Fax: 860-257-4125
Web: http://www.ctbar.org

Delaware State Bar Association
201 Orange Street, Suite 1100
Wilmington, DE 19801
Tel: 302-658-5279, Fax: 302-658-5212
Web: http://www.dsba.org

District of Columbia Bar Association
1819 H Street, NW, 12th FL
Washington, DC 20006-3690
Tel: 202-223-6600, Fax: 202-293-3388
Web: http://www.dcbar.org

Florida State Bar Association
650 Apalachee Parkway
Tallahassee, FL 32399-2300
Tel: 904-561-5600, Fax: 904-561-5827
Web: http://www.FLABAR.org

Georgia State Bar
800 The Hurt Building
50 Hurt Plaza, Atlanta, GA 30303
Tel: 800-334-6865, Fax: 404-527-8717
Web: http://www.gabar.org

Hawaii State Bar Association
Penthouse 1, 9th Floor
1136 Union Mall, Honolulu HI 96813
Tel: 808-537-1868, Fax: 808-521-7936
Web: http://www.hsba.org

Idaho State Bar
P.O. Box 895
525 W Jefferson Street
Boise, ID 83701
Tel: 208-334-4500, Fax: 208-334-4515
Web: http://www2.state.id.ud/isb/

Illinois State Bar Association
424 S. Second Street
Springfield, IL 62701
Tel: 217-525-1760, Fax: 217-525-0712
Web: http://www.illinoisbae.org

Indiana State Bar Association
230 E. Ohio, 4th Floor
Indiana Bar Center
Indianapolis, IN 46204-2199
Tel: 317-639-5465, Fax: 317-266-2588
Web: http://www.state.in.us/judiciary/ble

Iowa State Bar Association
521 E. Locust, Suite 300
Des Moines, IA 50309-1939
Tel: 515-243-3179, Fax: 515-243-2511
Web: http://www.iowabar.org/

Kansas State Bar Association
P.O. Box 1037
1200 Harrison Street
Topeka, KS 66612
Tel: 913-234-5696, Fax: 913-234-3813
Web: http://www.iowabar.org

Kentucky Bar Association
514 West Main Street
Frankfurt, KY 40601-1883
Tel: 502-564-3795, Fax: 502-564-3225
Web: http://www.kybar.org

Louisiana State Bar Association
601 St. Charles Avenue
New Orleans, LA, 70130
Tel: 504-566-1600, Fax: 504-566-0930
Web: http://www.lsba.org

Maine State Bar Association
P.O. Box 788
124 State Street Augusta, ME 04330
Tel: 207-622-7523, Fax: 207-623-0083
Web: http://www.mainebar.org

Maryland State Bar Association
520 W. Fayette Street
Baltimore, MD, 21201
Tel: 410-685-7878, Fax: 410-837-0518
Web: http://www.msba.org

Massachusetts Bar Association
20 West Street
Boston, MA 02111-1218
Tel: 617-338-0500, Fax: 617-338-0650
Web: http://www.massbar.org

Michigan State Bar Association
306 Townsend Street
Lansing, MI 48933-2083
Tel: 517-372-9030, Fax: 517-372-2410
Web: http://www.michbar.org

Minnesota State Bar Association
514 Nicollet Mall, Suite 300
Minneapolis, MN 55402
Tel: 612-333-1183, Fax: 612-333-4927
Web: http://www.mnbar.org

The Mississippi Bar
P.O. Box 2168
643 N. State Street Jackson
MS, 39225-2168
Tel: 601-948-4471, Fax: 601-355-8635
Web: http://www.msbar.org

Missouri State Bar Association
326 Monroe
Jefferson City, MO 65102
Tel: 314-635-4128, Fax: 314-635-2811
Web: http://www.mobar.org

Montana - State Bar of Montana
P.O. Box 577
46 N. Last Chance Gulch, Suite 2A
Helena, MT 59624
Tel: 406-442-7660, Fax: 406-442-7763
Web: http://www.montanabar.org

Nebraska State Bar Association
P.O. Box 81809
635 S. 14th Street, 2nd Floor
Lincoln, NE 68501
Tel: 402-475-7091, Fax: 402-475-7098
Web: http://www.nebar.com

State Bar of Nevada
600 E. Charleston Blvd.
Las Vegas, NV, 89104
Tel: 702-382-2200, Fax: 702-385-2878
Web: http://www.nvbar.org

New Hampshire State Bar Association
112 Pleasant Street
Concord, NH 03301
Tel: 603-224-6942, Fax: 603-224-2910
Web: http://www.nhbar.org

New Jersey State Bar Association
New Jersey Law Center
One Constitution Square
New Brunswick, NJ 08901-1500
Tel: 732-249-5000, Fax: 732-249-2815
Web: http://www.njsba.com

New Mexico - State Bar of New Mexico
P.O. Box 25883
121 Tijeras Street NE
Albuquerque, NM, 87102
Tel: 505-842-6132, Fax: 505-843-8765
Web: http://www.technet.nm.org/sbnm/

New York State Bar Association
One Elk Street
Albany, NY 12207
Tel: 518-487-5557, Fax: 518-487-5564
Web: http://www.nysba.org

North Carolina State Bar Association
800 Weston Pkwy
Cary, NC 27519
Tel: 919-677-0561, Fax: 919-677-0761
Web: http://www.barlinc.org

North Carolina State Bar
208 Fayetteville Street Mall
Raleigh, NC 27601
Tel: 919-828-4620, Fax: 919-821-9168
Web: http://www.ncbar.com

State Bar Association of North Dakota
P.O. Box 2136
Bismarck, ND 58502-2136
Tel: 701-255-1404, Fax: 701-224-1621
Web: http://www.court.stste.nd.us

Ohio State Bar Association
P.O. Box 1562
1700 Lake Shore Drive
Columbus, OH 43216-6562
Tel: 614-487-2050, Fax: 614-487-1008
Web: http://www.ohiobar.org

Oklahoma Bar Association
1901 N. Lincoln
Oklahoma City, OK 73105
Tel: 405-524-2365, Fax: 405-524-1115
Web: http://www.okbar.org

Oregon State Bar
5200 SW Meadows Road
Lake Oswego, OR 97035
Tel: 503-620-0222, Fax: 503-684-1366
Web: http://www.osbar.org

Pennsylvania State Bar Association
P.O. Box 186
100 South Street
Harrisburg, PA 17108-0186
Tel: 717-238-6715, Fax: 717-238-1204
Web: http://www.pa-bar.org

Puerto Rico Bar Association
P.O. Box 1900
San Juan, PR 00902
Tel: 809-721-3358, Fax: 809-725-0330
Web: http://www.tribunalpr.org

Rhode Island State Bar Association
115 Cedar Street
Providence RI 02903
Tel: 401-421-5740, Fax: 401-421-2703
Web: http://www.ribar.com

South Carolina Bar
P.O. Box 608
950 Taylor Street
Columbia, SC 29202
Tel: 803-799-6653, Fax: 803-799-4118
Web: http://www.scbar.org

South Dakota State Bar Association
222 E. Capitol
Pierre, SD 57501
Tel: 605-224-7554, Fax: 605-224-0282
Web: http://www.sdbar.org

Tennessee Bar Association
622 West End Avenue
Nashville, TN 37205-2403
Tel: 615-383-7421, Fax: 615-297-8058
Web: http://www.tba.org

State Bar of Texas
P.O. Box 12487
1414 Colorado
Austin, TX 78711-2487
Tel: 512-463-1463, Fax: 512- 473-2295
Web: http://www.texasbar.com

Utah State Bar
645 S. 200 East
Salt Lake City, UT 84111-3834
Tel: 801-531-9077, Fax: 801-531-0660
Web: http://www.utahbar.org

Vermont State Bar Association
P.O. Box 100
35-37 Court Street
Montpelier, VT 05602
Tel: 802-223-2020, Fax: 802-223-1573
Web: http://www.vtbar.org

Virgin Islands Bar Association
P.O. Box 4108
Christiansted, USVI 00822
Tel: 809-778-7497, Fax: 809-773-5060
Web: http://www.vibar.org

Virginia State Bar
707 E. Main Street, Suite 1500
Richmond, VA 23219-2803
Tel: 804-775-0500, Fax: 804-775-0501
Web: http://www.vsb.org

Washington State Bar Association
500 Westin Bldg
2001 6th Avenue
Seattle, WA 98121-2599
Tel: 206-727-8200, Fax: 206-727-8320
Web: http://www.wsba.org

West Virginia State Bar Association
2006 Kanawha Boulevard East
Charleston, WV 25311
Tel: 304-558-2456, Fax: 304-558-2467
Web: http://www.wvbar.org

Wisconsin State Bar Association
402 W. Wilson
Madison, WI 53703
Tel: 608-250-6101, Fax: 608-257-5502
Web: http://www.wisbar.org/home.htm

Wyoming State Bar
P.O. Box 109
500 Randall Avenue
Cheyenne, WY 82001
Tel: 307-632-9061, Fax: 307-632-3737
Web: http://www.wyoming.org

Appendix B

List of Foreign Bar Associations

Supranational Associations

International Bar Association
271 Regent Street
London W1B 2AQ UK
Tel: +44 (0) 20 7629 1206, Fax: +44 (0) 20 7409 0456
E-mail: http://www.ibanet.org/
Web: member@int-bar.org

NATIONAL ASSOCIATIONS

United Kingdom
Law Society of England & Wales

113 Chancery Lane
London WC2A 1PL UK
Tel: +44 20 7242 1222
E-mail: enquiries@lawsoc.org.uk
Web: www.lawsoc.org.uk

The General Council of the Bar
2/3 Cursitor Street
London EC4A 1NE, England, UK
Tel: + 44-171-440 4000
Web: www.barcouncil.org.uk/

Ireland

Honorable Society of King's Inns
Herietta Street
Dublin 1, Ireland
Tel: 353 1 874 4840, Fax: 353 1 872 6048
E-mail: info@kingsinns.ie
Web: http://www.iol.ie/kingsinns/

Law Society of Ireland
Blackhall Place
Dublin 7, Ireland
Tel: 353 1 672 4802, Fax: 353 1 672 4992
E-mail: info@lawsociety.ie
Web: http://www.lawsociety.ie/

CARIBBEAN

Bahamas Bar Association
P.O. Box N-4632
Nassau, Bahamas
Tel: 1-242-326-3276
E-mail: Not Available
Web: Not Available

Barbados Bar Association
P.O. Box 773
Bridgetown, Barbados.
Tel: 1 246 437 7316
E-mail: Not Available
Web: Not Available

Bermuda Bar Association
P.O. Box HM 125
Hamilton, HM AX, Bermuda
Tel: 809-295-4540, Fax: 809-295-4540
E-mail: Not Available
Web: Not Available

Cayman Islands Law Society
P.O. Box 309
Grand Cayman, Cayman Island
Tel: 809-949-8066, Fax: 809-949-8080
E-mail: Not Available
Web: Not Available

Jamaican Bar Association
78-80 Harbour Street
Kingston, Jamaica
Tel: 809-922-2319, Fax: 809-967-3783
E-mail: Not Available
Web: Not Available

ASIA AND PACIFIC RIM

The Law Society of Hong Kong
3rd Floor, Wing on House
71 Des Voeux Road
Central, Hong Kong
Tel: 852-28460500, Fax: 852-28450387
E-mail: adadmin@hklawsoc.org.hk
Web: http://www.hklawsoc.org.hk/pub/

The Law Society of Singapore
39 South Bridge Road
Singapore 058673
Tel: 6538-2500 Fax: 6533-5700
E-mail: lawsoc@lawsoc.org.sg
Web: http://www.lawsociety.org.sg/

The New Zealand Law Society
P.O. Box 5041
26 Waring Taylor Street
Wellington, New Zealand, DX SP20202.
Tel: +64 4 472 7837 Fax: +64 4 473 7909
E-mail: inquiries@lawyers.org.nz
Web: http://www.nz-lawsoc.org.nz/

National Bar Association of Bangladesh
57/2 Central Road, Dhanmondi
Dhaka, 1205, Bangladesh
Tel:880 2933 7695, Fax: 880 283 9427
E-mail: Not Available
Web: Not Available

Hong Kong Bar Association
The Supreme Court, LG/2 Floor
Queensway, 38, Hong Kong
Tel: 852-2869-0210, Fax: 852-2869-0189
E-mail: info@hkba.org
Web: www.hkba.org

Appendix C

List of ABA Law Schools Offering LL.M Degree Programs

Alabama

University of Alabama, School of Law
Law School Admissions Office
Box 870382
Tuscaloosa, AL 35487-0382
Tel: 205-348-5440, Fax: 205-348-3194
E-mail: admissions@law.ua.edu
Web: www.law.ua.edu
LL.M Programs:
    Taxation
    Master of Laws for International Students

Samford University, Cumberland School of Law
800 Lakeshore Drive
Birmingham, AL 35229
Tel: 205-726-2702, Fax: 205-726-2673
E-mail: lawadmissions@samford.edu
Web: www.samford.edu/schools/law.html
LL.M Programs:
    Master of Laws, General

Arizona

University of Arizona, School of Law
P.O. Box 210176
Tucson, AZ 85721
Tel: 520-621-3477, Fax: 520-621-9140
E-mail: admissions@nt.law.arizona.edu
Web: www.law.arizona.edu
LL.M Programs: :

International Trade Law
Indigenous Peoples Law & Policy

Arkansas

University of Arkansas, School of Law
Leflar Law Center
WATR 203
Fayetteville, AR 72701-1201
Tel: 501-575-3102
E-mail: admissions@uark.edu
Web: http://law.uark.edu
LL.M Programs:
Agricultural Law

California

University of California, Berkeley, School of Law
354 Boalt Hall
Berkeley, CA 94720-7200
Tel: 510-642-2274, Fax: 510-643-6222
E-mail: admission@law.berkeley.edu
Web: www.law.berkeley.edu
LL.M Programs:
Master of Laws, General

Whittier Law School
3333 Harbor Blvd.
Costa Mesa, CA 92626
Tel: 800-808-8188, Fax: 714-444-0250
E-mail: info@law.whittier.edu
Web: www.law.whittier.edu
LL.M Programs:
U.S. Legal Studies for Foreign Lawyers

University of California, Davis, School of Law
LL.M. Program
University Extension Building
Davis, CA 95616-4852
Tel: 530-752-6477
E-mail: lawadmissions@ucdavis.edu
Web: www.kinghall.ucdavis.edu
LL.M Programs:
Master of Laws, General

Southwestern University, School of Law
675 S. Westmoreland Ave.
Los Angeles, CA 90005
Tel: 213-738-6717, Fax: 213-383-1688
E-mail: admissions@swlaw.edu
Web: www.swlaw.edu
LL.M Programs:
      Entertainment and Media Law

University of California, Los Angeles (UCLA), School of Law
Office of Admissions
71 Dodd Hall
Box 951445
Los Angeles, CA 90095-1445
Tel: 310-825-2080, Fax: 310-825-9450
E-mail: admission@law.ucla.edu
Web: www.law.ucla.edu
LL.M Programs:
      Master of Laws, General

University of Southern California, School of Law
699 Exposition Blvd.
Los Angeles, CA 90089-0071
Tel: 213-821-5916, Fax: 213-821-5915
E-mail: llm@law.usc.edu
Web: http://lawweb.usc.edu/llm/
LL.M Programs:
      LLM Program for foreign graduate students

University of the Pacific, McGeorge School of Law
Admissions Office
3200 Fifth Avenue
Sacramento, CA 95817
Tel: 213-740-7331
E-mail: admissions@usc.edu/law
Web: www.usc.edu/law
LL.M Programs:
      Governmental Affairs
      International Water Resources Law
      Transnational Business Practice

California Western School of Law
225 Cedar Street
San Diego
CA 92101
Tel: 619-525-1401, Fax: 619-615-1401
E-mail: rbriscoe@cwsl.edu
Web: www.cwsl.edu
LL.M Programs:
> Comparative Law
> Trial Advocacy

University of San Diego, School of Law
5998 Alcala Park
Warren Hall
San Diego, CA 92110-2492
Tel: 619-260-4528, Fax: 619-260-2218
E-mail: info@acusd.edu
Web: www.acusd.edu/usdlaw
LL.M Programs:
> LLM program in Taxation
> Business and Corporate Law
> International Law
> Comparative Law for International Lawyers

Golden Gate University, School of Law
536 Mission Street
San Francisco, CA 94105
Tel: 415-442-6630
E-mail: lawadmit@ggu.edu
Web: http://www.ggu.edu/schools/law/index.html
LL.M Programs:
> LLM program in Environmental Law
> Taxation
> Intelectual Property
> U.S. Legal Studies
> International Legal Studies

University of California, Hastings, College of the Law
200 McAllister Street
San Francisco, CA 94102-4978
Tel: 415-565-4623, Fax: 415-565-4863
E-mail: admiss@uchastings.edu
Web: www.uchastings.edu
LL.M Programs:
> LLM Program, General

University of San Francisco, College of Law
Office of Graduate Admissions
2130 Fulton Street
San Francisco, CA 94117-1080
Tel: 415-422-5555, Fax: 415-422-6433
E-mail: Not available
Web: www.usfca.edu/online/colleges/law.html
LL.M Programs:
> LLM program for International Lawyers
> Intellectual Property Law

Santa Clara University, School of Law
500 El Camino Real
Santa Clara, CA 95053
Tel: 408-554-4800, Fax: 408-554-7897
E-mail: lawadmission@scu.edu
Web: www.scu.edu/law
LL.M Programs:
> LL.M. in U.S. Law for Foreign Lawyers
> International and Comparative Law
> Intellectual Property

Stanford University, School of law
559 Nathan Abbott Way
Stanford, CA 94305-8610
Tel: 650-723-2465, Fax: 650-725-0253
E-mail: admissions@law.stanford.edu
Web: http://lawschool.stanford.edu/
LL.M Programs:
> Corporate Governance and Practice
> Law, Science & Technology

Colorado

University of Denver, School of Law
7039 E. 18th Ave.
Denver, CO 80220
Tel: 303-871-6000, Fax: 303-871-6378
E-mail: admissions@law.du.edu
Web: http://www.law.du.edu/
LL.M Programs:
> International Natural Resources
> American and Comparative Law
> Taxation

Connecticut

University of Connecticut, School of Law
55 Elizabeth Street
Hartford, CT 06105-2290
Tel: 860-570-5159, Fax: 860-570-5159
E-mail: admit@law.uconn.edu
Web: www.law.uconn.edu
LL.M Programs:
U.S. Legal Studies

Yale Law School
Box 208215
New Haven, CT 06520-8215
Tel: 203-432-4995
E-mail: admissions.law@yale.edu
Web: www.law.yale.edu
LL.M Programs:
Master of Laws, General

Delaware

Widener University, School of Law
4601 Concord Pike
Box 7474
Wilmington, DE 19885-9806
Tel: 302-477-2162, Fax: 302-477-2224
E-mail: lawadmissions@law.widener.edu
Web: www.widener.edu/law/law.html
LL.M Programs:
Corporate Law and Finance

District of Columbia

American University, Washington College of Law
4801 Massachusetts Ave, NW
Washington, DC 20016-8189
Tel: 202-274-4101, Fax: 202-274-4107
E-mail: wcladmit@wclamerican.edu
Web: www.wclamerican.edu
LL.M Programs:
International Legal Studies

George Washington University, School of Law
2000 H Street, NW
Washington, DC 20052
Tel: 202-994-6261
E-mail: grad@law.gwu.edu
Web: http://www.law.gwu.edu/
LL.M Programs:
> Environmental Law
> Intellectual Property Law, International and Comparative Law
> Government Procurement Law
> Litigation and Dispute Resolution

Georgetown University, School of Law
Law Center
600 New Jersey Avenue
Washington, DC 20001
Tel: 202-739-0648
E-mail: id@main.n/c.gu.edu
Web: www.law.gu.edu
LL.M Programs:
> International and Comparative Law
> Taxation, Securities and Financial Regulation
> International Legal Studies
> General LLM program

Howard University, School of Law
2900 Van Ness Street, NW
Washington, DC 20008
Tel: 202-806-8008, Fax: 202-806-8162
E-mail: admissions@law.howard.edu
Web: www.law.howard.edu
LL.M Programs:
> Comparative and International Law

Florida

University of Miami, School of Law
1311 Miller Drive
Coral Gables, Florida 33124-0221
Tel: 305-284-2523
E-mail: admissions@law.miami.edu
Web: www.law.miami.edu
LL.M Programs:
>   Taxation, Estate Planning
>   Comparative Law
>   Inter-American Law
>   International Law
>   Ocean and Coastal Law
>   Real Property Development

University of Florida, School of Law
Box 117622
Gainesville, FL 32611-7622
Tel: 352-392-2087
E-mail: patrick@law.ufl.edu
Web: www.law.ufl.edu
LL.M Programs:
>   Comparative Law, Taxation

Saint Thomas University, School of Law
16400 N.W.32nd Avenue
Miami, FL 33054-9913
Tel: 800-245-4569
E-mail: lamy@stu.edu
Web: www.stu.edu/law
LL.M Programs:
>   Intercultural Human Rights
>   International Taxation

Stetson University, School of law
Office of International Programs
1401-61st Street South
St. Petersburg, FL 33707-3299
Tel: 727-562-7802, Fax: 727-343-0136
E-mail: lawadmit@hermes.law.stetson.edu
Web: www.law.stetson.edu
LL.M Programs:
>   International Law & Business

Georgia

University of Georgia, School of Law
Athens, GA 30602-5211
Tel: 706-542-5191
E-mail: intlgrad@uga.edu
Web: http://www.lawsch.uga.edu/
LL.M Programs:
      Master of Laws, General

Emory University, School of Law
Gambrell Hall
1301 Clifton Road
Atlanta, GA 30322-2770
Tel: 404-727-6801, Fax: 404-727-2477
E-mail: jbale@law.emory.edu
Web: www.law.emory.edu
LL.M Programs:
      Master of Laws, General

Hawaii

University of Hawaii at Manoa
William S. Richardson School of Law
2515 Dole Street
Honolulu, HI 96822
Tel: 808-956-7966, Fax: 808-956-3813
E-mail: lawadm@hawaii.edu
Web: www.hawaii.edu/law
LL.M Programs:
      Master of Laws, General

Illinois

University of Illinois at Urbana, Champaign, College of Law
Office of Graduate and International Legal Studies
504 East Pennsylvania Avenue
Champaign, IL 61820
Tel: 217-244-6415, Fax: 217-244-1478
E-mail: admissions@law.uiuc.edu
Web: www.law.uiuc.edu
LL.M Programs:
      Anglo-American Law

University of Chicago, School of Law
1111 E. 60th Street
Chicago, IL 60637
Tel: 773-702-9484, Fax: 773-834-0942
E-mail: admissions@law.uchicago.edu
Web: www.uchicago.edu
LL.M Programs:
      Master of Laws, General

DePaul University, School of Law
25 East Jackson Boulevard
Chicago, IL 60604-2287
Tel: 800-428-7453
E-mail: lawinfo@wppost.depaul.edu
Web: www.law.depaul.edu
LL.M Programs:
      Health Law
      Tax Law

Kent School of Law
565 West Adams
Chicago, IL 60661-3691
Tel: 312-906-5020
E-mail: admit@kentlaw.edu
Web: www.kentlaw.edu
LL.M Programs:
      Taxation
      Financial Services Law
      International & Comparative Law

John Marshall Law School
315 South Plymouth Court
Chicago, IL 60604
Tel: 312-987-1406, Fax: 312-427-5136
E-mail: admissions@jmls.edu
Web: www.jmls.edu
LL.M Programs:
      Comparative Legal Studies
      Information Technology
      International Business & Trade
      Tax Law, Employee Benefits
      Intellectual Property
      Real Estate

Loyola University Chicago, School of Law
One East Pearson Street
Chicago, Illinois 60611
Tel: 312-915-7170, Fax: 312-915-7201
E-mail: law-admission@luc.edu
Web: www.luc.edu/schools/law
LL.M Programs:
>Child and Family Law
>Business Law
>Health Law

Northwestern University, School of Law
357 East Chicago Avenue
Chicago, IL 60611-3069
Tel: 312-503-8465, Fax: 312-503-0178
E-mail: nubwadm@mwu.edu
Web: www.law.nwu.edu
LL.M Programs:
>Master of Laws, General
>Graduate Program in Law and Business

Indiana
Indiana University, School of Law
Bloomington, IN 47405-1001
Tel: 812-855-4765, Fax: 812-855-0555
E-mail: lawadmis@indiana.edu
Web: www.law.indiana.edu
LL.M Programs:
>Master of Laws, General

University of Notre Dame School of Law
P.O. Box 959
Notre Dame, IN 46556-0959
Tel: 219-631-6626, Fax: 219-631-3980
E-mail: lawbulletin@nd.edu
Web: www.law.nd.edu
LL.M Programs:
>International Human Rights Law
>International and Comparative Law

Valparaiso University, School of Law
Wesemann Hall
Valparaiso, IN 46383
Tel: 219-465-7829, Fax: 219-465-7808
E-mail: heike.spahn@valpo.edu

Web: www.valpo.edu/law
LL.M Programs:
       LLM program for Foreign Lawyers

Iowa

University of Iowa, School of Law
 Melrose at Byington Street
Suite 203
6329 Freret Street
Iowa City, IA 52242
Tel: 319-335-9095, Fax: 319-335-9019
E-mail: law-admissions@uiowa.edu
Web: www.uiowa.edu
LL.M Programs:
       International and Comparative Law

Louisiana

Louisiana State University
Paul M. Hebert Law Center
Baton Rouge
Louisiana 70803-1000
Tel: 225-388-8646, Fax: 225-388-8647
E-mail: bloup@lsu.edu
Web: www.law.lsu.edu
LL.M Programs:
       Master of Civil Law (M.C.L.)
       Master of Laws, General

Tulane University, School of Law
Weinmann Hall
Suite 203
6329 Freret Street
New Orleans, LA 70118
Tel: 504-865-5930, Fax: 504-865-6710
E-mail: admissions@tulane.edu
Web: www.law.tulane.edu
LL.M Programs:
       General LLM program
       International and Comparative Law
       Admiralty Law
       Energy and Environmental Law

Massachusetts

Boston University, School of Law
Office of Foreign Programs
765 Commonwealth Ave
Room 1240
Boston, MA 02215
Tel: 617-353-3100
E-mail: bulawadm@bu.edu
Web: www.bu.edu/law
LL.M Programs:
American Law
Banking Law
Tax Law

Harvard Law School
1563 Massachusetts Avenue
Cambridge, MA 02138
Tel: 617-495-3109, Fax: 617-495-1110
E-mail: admiss@law.harvard.edu
Web: www.law.harvard.edu
LL.M Programs:
Master of Laws, General

Michigan

Thomas M. Cooley Law School
PO Box 13038
Lansing, MI 48901
Tel: 517-371-5140 ext. 2241, Fax: 517-334-5718
E-mail: admissions@cooley.edu
Web: www.cooley.edu/llm/index.htm
LL.M Programs:
Master of Laws, Intelectual Property
Master of Laws, Taxation

University of Michigan, School of Law
625 South State Street
Ann Arbor, MI 48109-1210
Tel: 734-764-1358
E-mail: law.grad.admission@umich.edu
Web: www.law.umich.edu/
LL.M Programs:
Master of Laws, General

Master of Laws by Research
Master of Comparative Law (M.C.L.)

Wayne State University, School of Law
471 West Palmer
Detroit, MI 48202
Tel: 313-577-3937, Fax: 313-577-6000
E-mail: lindasims@wayne.edu
Web: www.wayne.edu
LL.M Programs:
Taxation
Labor Law
Corporate and Finance Law

Minnesota

Hamline University, School of Law
1536 Hewitt Avenue
Saint Paul, MN 55104
Tel: 651-523-2461, Fax: 651-523-6000
E-mail: lawadm@gw.hamline.edu
Web: www.hamline.edu
LL.M Programs:
LLM program for International Lawyers

University of Minnesota, School of Law
229-19th Avenue South
Minneapolis, MN 55455
Tel: 612-625-1000, Fax: 612-626-1874
E-mail: umnlsadm@tc.umn.edu
Web: http://www.law.umn.edu/
LL.M Programs:
LLM program for Foreign Lawyers

Missouri

University of Missouri-Columbia, School of Law
103 Hulston Hall
Columbia, MO 65211
Tel: 573-882-6042, Fax: 573-882-9625
E-mail: umclawadmissions@missouri.edu
Web: www.law.missouri.edu
LL.M Programs:
Dispute Resolution

University of Missouri, Kansas City, School of Law
5100 Rockhill Road
Kansas City, MO 64110-2499
Tel: 816-235-1644, Fax: 816-235-5276
E-mail: klosterman@umkc.edu
Web: www.law.umkc.edu
LL.M Programs:
    Taxation
    Master of Laws, General

Saint Louis University, School of Law
3700 Lindell Boulevard
Saint Louis, MO 63108
Tel: 314-997-2800
E-mail: admissions@law.slu.edu
Web: www.law.slu.edu
LL.M Programs:
    Health Law
    LLM program for Foreign Lawyers

Washington University, School of Law
Campus Box 1120
One Brookings Drive
St. Louis, MO 63130-4899
Tel: 314-935-4525, Fax: 314-935-6959
E-mail: admiss@walaw.wash.edu
Web: http://ls.wash.edu
LL.M Programs:
    Taxation
    Intellectual Property Law
    LLM program for International lawyers

Nebraska

University of Nebraska, School of Law
Ross McCollum Hall
P.O. Box 830902
Lincoln, NE 65883-0902
Tel: 402-472-2161, Fax: 402-472-5185
E-mail: lawadm.unlinfo@unl.edu
Web: www.unl.edu/lawcoll
LL.M Programs:
    Master of Legal Studies (M.L.S.)

New Hampshire

Franklin Pierce Law Center
2 White Street
Concord, NH 03301
Tel: 603-228-9217, Fax: 603-228-1074
E-mail: l.admissions@fplc.edu
Web: www.fplc.edu
LL.M Programs:
> Intellectual Property Law

New York

State University of New York at Buffalo, School of Law
John Lord O'Brian Hall
Buffalo, NY 14260
Tel: 716-645-2052
E-mail: law-admissions@buffalo.edu
Web: http://www.law.buffalo.edu/
LL.M Programs:
> Criminal Law

Cornell University, School of Law
240 Myron Taylor Hall
Ithaca, NY 14853-4901
Tel: 607-255-5141, Fax: 607-255-7193
E-mail: lawadmit@postoffice.law.cornell.edu
Web: http://www.lawschool.cornell.edu/
LL.M Programs:
> American Domestic Law
> International Law
> Comparative Law

Hofstra University, School of Law
Hempstead, NY 11549
Tel: 516-463-5916, Fax: 516-463-6264
E-mail: lawpts@hofstra.edu
Web: www.hofstra.edu/law
LL.M Programs:
> American Legal Studies
> International Law

Columbia University, School of Law
Office of Graduate Programs
435 West 116th Street

New York, NY 10027-7297
Tel: 212-854-2670
E-mail: Admissions@law.columbia.edu
Web: www.law.columbia.edu
LL.M Programs:
    Master of Laws, General

Fordham University, School of Law
140 West 62nd Street
New York, NY 10023
Tel: 212-636-6883, Fax: 212-636-6922
E-mail: llm@law.fordham.edu
Web: http://law.fordham.edu/llmprogram.htm
LL.M Programs:
    Banking
    Corporate and Finance Law
    International Business and Trade Law

New York University, School of Law
40 Washington Square South
Vanderbilt Hall
New York, NY 10012-1074
Tel: 212-998-6060, Fax: 212-995-4527
E-mail: admissions@nyu.edu
Web: www.law.nyu.edu
LL.M Programs:
    Master of Laws, General
    Comparative Jurisprudence
    Corporation Law
    International Legal Studies
    International Taxation
    Labor & Employment Law
    Public Service Law
    Taxation
    Trade Regulation

Yeshiva University, Cardozo School of Law
55 Fifth Avenue
New York, NY 10003
Tel: 212-790-0274, Fax: 212-790-0482
E-mail: lawinfo@ymail.yu.edu
Web: www.cardozo.yu.edu
LL.M Programs:
    Intellectual Property
    Master of Laws, General

Pace University, School of Law
78 North Broadway
White Plains, NY 10603
Tel: 914-422-4010, Fax: 914-422-4248
E-mail: adagostino@genesis.law.pace.edu
Web: www.pace.edu/law
LL.M Programs:
>Environmental Law
>Comparative Law

Touro Law School
300 Nassau Road
Huntington, NY 11743
Tel: 516-421-2244
E-mail: admissions@tourolaw.edu
Web: www.tourolaw.edu
LL.M Programs:
>Master of Laws, General

North Carolina

Duke University, School of Law
P.O. Box 90362
Durham, NC 27708
Tel: 916-613-7020, Fax: 916-613-7257
E-mail: admissions@law.duke.edu
Web: www.duke.edu/law
LL.M Programs:
>International and Comparative Law

Wake Forest University, School of Law
P.O. Box 7206
Reynolda Station
Winston-Salem, NC 27109
Tel: 336-758-5430
E-mail: llm-admissions@law.wfu.edu
Web: http://www.law.wfu.edu/
LL.M Programs:
>American Law

Ohio

Case Western Reserve University, School of Law
11075 East Boulevard
Cleveland, OH 44106-7148
Tel: 216-368-3600, Fax: 216-368-6144
E-mail: lawadmissions@po.cwru.edu
Web: www.law.cwru.edu
LL.M Programs:
>LLM program in United States Legal Studies for Foreign Lawyers
>Taxation

Oregon

Lewis and Clark College, School of Law
10015 S.W. Terwilliger Boulevard
Portland
OR 97219-7799
Tel: 503-768-6613, Fax: 503-768-6671
E-mail: lawadmissions@lclark.edu
Web: www.lclark.edu/law
LL.M Programs:
>Master of Laws, General

Pennsylvania

Pennsylvania State University, Dickinson School of Law
150 South College Street
Carlisle, PA 17013-2899
Tel: 717-240-5207, Fax: 717-240-3503
E-mail: dsladmit@psu.edu
Web: www.dsl.edu
LL.M Programs:
>Master of Laws, General

University of Pennsylvania, School of Law
The Admissions Office
3400 Chestnut Street
Philadelphia, PA 19104-6204
Tel: 215-898-7400
E-mail: admissions@oyez.law.upenn.edu
Web: www.law.upenn.edu
LL.M Programs:
>Master of Laws, General
>Master of Comparative Law

Temple University, James E. Basley School of Law
1719 North Broad St.
Philadelphia, PA 19104-6204
Tel: 215-204-8925, Fax: 215-204-1185
E-mail: lawadmis@blue.temple.edu
Web: www.temple.edu/lawschool
LL.M Programs:
        LL.M program for International Lawyers
        Trial Advocacy
        Transnational Law
        Taxation, Master of Laws

University of Pittsburgh, School of Law
3900 Forbes Avenue
Pittsburgh, PA 19104-6204
Tel: 412-648-1412, Fax: 412-648-2647
E-mail: admissions@law.pitt.edu
Web: www.pitt.law.edu
LL.M Programs:
        LLM program for Foreign Law Graduates

Tennessee

Vanderbilt University, School of Law
131 21st Ave. South
Nashville, TN 37203-1181
Tel: 615-322-6452
E-mail: admissions@law. vanderbilt.edu
Web: http://law.vanderbilt.edu/
LL.M Programs:
        LL.M. Program for Foreign Lawyers

Texas

University of Texas, School of Law
727 East Dean Keeton Street
Austin TX 78741
Tel: 512-232-1200, Fax: 512-471-6988
E-mail: admissions@utexas.edu
Web: www.utexas.edu/law
LL.M Programs:
        LLM program for Foreign Lawyers
        Latin American & International Law

Southern Methodist University, School of Law
P.O. Box 750110
Dallas
TX 75275-0110
Tel: 214-768-2550, Fax: 214-768-2549
E-mail: admissions@smu.edu
Web: www.smu.edu/law
LL.M Programs:
    Taxation
    International & Comparative Law
    Master of Laws, General

University of Houston, School of law
Houston, TX 77204-6060
Tel: 713-743-1070, Fax: 713-743-2194
E-mail: admissions@law.uh.edu
Web: www.law.uh.edu
LL.M Programs:
    Environment and Natural Resources Law
    Energy
    Health Law
    Intellectual Property Law
    International Economic Law
    Taxation

Utah

University of Utah, School of Law
332 South 1400 East Front
Salt Lake City, UT 84112-0730
Tel: 801-581-7479, Fax: 801-581-6897
E-mail: gormley@law.utah.edu
Web: www.law.utah.edu
LL.M Programs:
    Natural Resource and Environmental Law

Virginia

University of Virginia, School of Law
580 Massie Road
Charlottesville, VA 22903-1789
Tel: 804-924-7351
E-mail: lawadmit@virginia.edu
Web: www.law.virginia.edu

LL.M Programs:
> Master of Laws, General

College of William and Mary, School of Law
P.O. Box 8795
Williamsburg, VA 23187
Tel: 757-221-3785, Fax: 757-221-3261
E-mail: lawadm@wm.edu
Web: www.wm.edu/law
LL.M Programs:
> American Law

Vermont

Vermont Law School, School of Law
P.O. Box 96
Chelsea Street
South Royalton, VT 05068-0096
Tel: 802-763-8303, Fax: 802-763-7071
E-mail: admiss@vermontlaw.edu
Web: www.vermontlaw.edu
LL.M Programs:
> Environmental Law

Washington

University of Washington, School of Law
1100 N.E. Campus Parkway
Seattle, WA 98105-6617
Tel: 206-543-2283
E-mail: swinehar@u.washington.edu
Web: http://www.law.washington.edu/
LL.M Programs:
> Taxation
> Asian and Comparative Law
> Law of Sustainable International Development
> Intellectual Property and Technology Law

Wisconsin

University of Wisconsin, School of Law
975 Bascom Mall
Madison WI 53706-1399
Tel: 608-262-5914, Fax: 608-262-5485
E-mail: admissions@law.wisc.edu
Web: www.law.wisc.edu
LL.M Programs:
      Master of Laws, General

Appendix D

Other Programs and Books

Bar Review Programs Programs

America's Guaranteed Bar Review (Both Baby Bar & General Bar)
725 J Street
Sacramento, CA 95814
Tel: 800-359-8010
Web: http://www.americaslegalbookstore.com

Gallagher New York Bar Exam Essay/MPT Training Schools
A Division of Mary Campbell Gallagher & Co., Inc.
P.O. BOX 1308
Gracie Station
New York, NY 10028
(212) 327-2817
Web: www.BarWrite.com

BarBri Bar Review
Web: http://www.barbri.com/

Fleming's Fundamentals of Law (Both Baby Bar & General Bar)
23166 Los Alisos Blvd., Suite 238
Mission Viejo, CA 92691-2843
Tel: 949-770-7030
Web: http://www.lawprepare.com/

PasstheBar.com (Both Baby Bar & General Bar)
12 25th Avenue # 3
Venice, CA 90291
Tel: 310-699-6891
Web: www.passthebar.com

PMBR Multistate Specialist
Tel: 800-523-0777 or 800-315-1735
Email: info@pmbr.com
Web: http://www.pmbr.com/

Great Books Available at: www.MariluxPress.com

LSAT Books (*If you really want to take it* after all you just learned)

- **Master the LSAT** - Jeff Kolby

- **Kaplan LSAT 180** - Kaplan

Books About Getting In (*And Staying In*) **ABA Law Schools**

- **How to Get into the Top Law Schools** - Richard Montauk, JD

- **Law School Insider** - Jeremy B. Horwitz

- **Law School Confidential** – Robert H. Miller

British Law

- **The British Lawyer: Clarifying the Misconceptions** – Mr. Kulwant Singh Boora

Bar Review Books

- **How to Study For The Bar Exam In Three Days** – Erik J. Heels
  This is a book about time and information management. I don't recommend anyone wait until three days before the Bar exam to start studying…but if you're in a crisis situation, Eric Heels gives some good advice on how to make the best use of limited time. Incidentally, the principles learned in this book are applicable even if you have more than 3 days to prepare.

- **Scoring High on Bar Exam Essays** – Mary Campbell Gallagher
  Simply the best Bar Exam essay book around.

- **Bar Exam Secrets**
  25 Things You Can Do Right Now To Dramatically Increase Your Chances Of Passing Any Bar Exam– Peter J. Loughlin

CLEP Books and Programs

- **CLEP Success 2003** - Peterson's

- **The Best Test Preparation for CLEP** - Joseph A. Alvarez

- **The Best Review for the CLEP General.Exams** - Michael V. Angrosino

Sources for New and Used Textbooks

- **www.MaxStudy.com**

- **www.BaristerBooks.com**

- **Americas Legal Bookstore**
  725 J Street
  Sacramento, CA 95814
  Tel: 800-359-8010
  Web: http://www.americaslegalbookstore.com

- **eCampus**

- **Low Cost College Textbooks**.

- **Textbookx.com**

Appendix E

The Law School Bible Newsletter

To subscribe to my free periodic newsletter you must be a registered reader. Registration/subscription is free and I encourage you to do so if you haven't done so already. To register you need to send an e-mail to <u>register@LawSchoolBible.com</u>. You must include your first and last name and the words register/subscribe. You may unsubscribe at any time

What will you receive as a registered reader and subscriber?

- You will receive my periodic newsletter with articles by and about other students in alternative law-school programs.
- Sources of discount law textbooks and study materials
- The most current sources for grants, scholarships, and student loans.
- Links to other alternative law students wishing to form study groups.
- Special Reports on any changes in bar admission rules.
- Articles featuring the best alternative law programs.
- Special Reports on any changes in contact details for schools, tutorial programs, bar associations, etc.
- You can unsubscribe at any time…but don't.

Appendix F

Personal Consultation

This book was designed as a primer in alternative legal education. I have packed it with resources to save you hours, weeks, months and perhaps years of searching to find the right program and an understanding of the complexities of the bar-admission process. Take your time and read it carefully and you will likely find the solution to achieving your goal of becoming a lawyer. However, if you feel it necessary, you may contact me for a personal consultation for a reasonable fee.

Again, while I will be pleased to assist you, please be sure to read this book first. It is advised that you prepare your questions and submit them in writing prior to scheduling your personal consultation

To request a consultation please send an e-mail to:
Consultant@LawSchoolBible.com

To become a registered reader/subscriber send an e-mail to register@LawSchoolBible.com

Appendix G

List of Law Degrees

The following are among the usual law degrees conferred in common law countries. Incidentally, the Juris Doctor degree, a first law degree, is generally only conferred in the United States and has gained in popularity since the 1960s. It is not a terminal degree. One notable exception to this is that some Australian law schools have recently begun offering the J.D. as an advanced law degree.

First Law Degrees

LL.B.	Bachelor of Laws
J.D.	Juris Doctor*
B.C.L	Bachelor of Civil Laws

*Note: The Juris Doctor degree is deemed to be the academic equivalent of LL.B. degree. Also, the B.S.L. or Bachelor of Science of Laws is not a professional first law degree and is therefore excluded from this category.

Advanced Law Degrees

LL.M.	Master of Laws
M.C.L.	Master of Comparative Law
	Master of Civil Law
	Master of Common Law

Terminal Law Degrees

LL.D.	Doctor of Laws (Doctor Lugum)
	(Not generally used in the US)
S.J.D.	Doctor of Judicial Science
J.S.D.	Doctor of the Science of Law

About The Author

Author and attorney Peter Loughlin is an expert on non-traditional law school education. A former law enforcement officer with the City of New York, Loughlin "walks the talk"; he'd always wanted to become a lawyer, but family obligations and financial constraints prevented him from traveling the traditional route into the legal profession. Loughlin embarked on an alternative path using self-study and distance-learning programs, earning JD and LL.M degrees. After passing the Bar examination, he founded The Loughlin Law Firm, which specializes in Immigration and US federal law, and JurisConsults International Group, LLC, a legal consulting firm whose members are authors, professors and internationally-known economists and lawyers. To learn more about the author visit **www.PeterLoughlin.com**.

www.ingramcontent.com/pod-product-compliance
Lightning Source LLC
Chambersburg PA
CBHW021556210326
41599CB00010B/475